THE LIVING MOUNTAIN

Anna (Nan) Shepherd was born in 1893 and died in 1981. Closely attached to Aberdeen and her native Deeside, she graduated from her home university in 1915, and went to work for the next forty-one years as a lecturer in English at what is now Aberdeen College of Education. An enthusiastic gardener and hill walker, she made many visits to the Cairngorms with students and friends and was a keen member of the Deeside Field Club. *The Living Mountain* testifies to her love of the hills and her knowledge of them in all their moods. Her many further travels included visits to Norway, France, Italy, Greece and South Africa, but she always returned to the house where she was raised and lived almost all her adult life, in the village of West Cults, three miles from Aberdeen on North Deeside.

Also by Nan Shepherd

The Quarry Wood
The Weatherhouse
A Pass In The Grampians
In The Cairngorms
Wild Geese: A Collection of Nan Shepherd's Writing

THE LIVING MOUNTAIN

NAN SHEPHERD

INTRODUCED BY
ROBERT MACFARLANE

AFTERWORD BY
JEANETTE WINTERSON

CANONGATE

This Canons edition published in Great Britain, the USA and Canada
in 2014 by Canongate Books

Distributed in the USA by Publishers Group West and
in Canada by Publishers Group Canada

First published in Great Britain in 1977 by Aberdeen University Press

Published as part of *The Grampian Quartet* in 1996 by Canongate Books Ltd,
14 High Street, Edinburgh EH1 1TE

canongate.co.uk

21

British Library Cataloguing-in-Publication Data
A catalogue record for this book is available on
request from the British Library

ISBN 978 0 85786 183 2

Typeset in Goudy by Palimpsest Book Production Ltd,
Falkirk, Stirlingshire

Printed and bound in Great Britain by Clays Ltd, Elcograf S.p.A.

CONTENTS

THE
CAIRNGORM PLATEAU

WITH SOME PEAKS
AND PLACES

N

GRANTOWN ON SPEY

River Spey

BOAT OF GARTEN

Loch Garten

AVIEMORE

Loch an Uaine

Loch Morlich

*Loch an
Eilein*

Cairn Gorm ▲

Loch Avon

*Loch Coire
an Lochain*

Lairig Ghru

*Sgoran
Dubh* ▲

*Ben
a'Bhuird* ▲

Ben Avon ▲

*Poots
of Dee*

*Loch
Etchachan*

Braeriach ▲

*Loch
Einich*

*Wells
of Dee*

*Ben
MacDhui* ▲

*Dubh
Loch*

River Feshie

Garbh Choire

River Avon

Cairntoul ▲

*Derry
Lodge*

Quoich

BRAEMAR

Slugain

*Beinn
Bhrotain* ▲

INVEREY

River Dee

Morrone ▲

10 Kilometres / 6.2 Miles

INTRODUCTION

by Robert Macfarlane

The Cairngorm Mountains of north-east Scotland are Britain's Arctic. In winter, storm winds of up to 170 miles per hour rasp the upper shires of the range, avalanches scour its slopes and northern lights flare green and red above the summits. Even in high summer, snow still lies in the deepest corries, sintering slowly into ice. Year-round the wind is so insistent that on the plateaux there are bonsai pines, fully grown at six inches, and juniper bushes which flatten themselves across the rocks to form densely woven dwarf forests. Two of Scotland's great rivers – the Dee and the Avon – have their sources here: falling as rain, filtered by rock, pooling as the clearest water into which I have ever looked and then running seawards with gathering strength. The range itself is the eroded stump of a mass of magma that rose up through the earth's crust in the Devonian period, cooled into granite, then emerged out of the surrounding schists and gneiss. The Cairngorms were once higher than today's Alps, but over millions of years they have been eroded into a low-slung wilderness of whale-backed hills and shattered cliffs. Born of fire, carved by ice, finessed with wind, water and snow, the massif is a terrain shaped by what Nan Shepherd – in this slender masterpiece about the region – calls 'the elementals'.

Anna (Nan) Shepherd was born near Aberdeen in 1893 and died there in 1981, and during her long life she spent hundreds of days and thousands of miles exploring the Cairngorms on foot. Her reputation as a writer rests chiefly on her three modernist novels – *The Quarry Wood*, *The Weatherhouse*, *A Pass in the Grampians* – but to my mind her most important prose work has until recently been her least-known: *The Living Mountain*, which she wrote during the last years of the Second World War.

Shepherd was localist of the best kind: she came to know her chosen place closely, but that closeness served to intensify rather than to limit her vision. She had a modest middle-class upbringing and a modestly regional life: she attended Aberdeen High School for Girls, graduated from Aberdeen University in 1915 and worked for the subsequent forty-one years as a lecturer in English at what is now the Aberdeen College of Education (wryly describing her teacherly role there as the 'heaven-appointed task of trying to prevent a few of the students who pass through our Institution from conforming altogether to the approved pattern'). She travelled widely – including to Norway, France, Italy, Greece and South Africa – but only ever lived in the village of West Cults on north Deeside. The Cairngorms, whose foothills rise a few miles from West Cults, were her heartland. Into and out of those mountains she went in all seasons, by dawn, day, dusk and night, walking sometimes alone, and sometimes with friends, students or fellow walkers from the Deeside Field Club. Like all true mountain-lovers, she got altitude sickness if she spent too long at sea-level.

From a young age, Shepherd was hungry for life. She seems

to have lived with a great but quiet gusto. Writing to a friend about a photograph of herself as a toddler on her mother's knee, she describes herself as 'all movement, legs and arms flailing as though I were demanding to get at life – I swear those limbs move as you look at them'. Intellectually, she was what Coleridge once called a 'library-cormorant'; omnivorous and voracious in her reading. On 7 May 1907, aged just fourteen, she started the first of what she called her 'medleys' – commonplace books into which she copied literary, religious and philosophical citations, and which reveal the breadth of her reading as a young woman.

Shepherd published her three novels in an extraordinary five-year burst of creativity between 1928 and 1933. Hard on their heels came a collection of poetry titled *In The Cairngorms*, which was published in 1934 in a tiny print run and is now almost impossible to find. It was the book of which she was most proud. Shepherd had a clear genre hierarchy in her mind, and poetry was at its pinnacle. 'Poetry', she wrote to the novelist Neil Gunn (with whom she had a flirty and intellectually ardent correspondence), holds 'in intensest being the very heart of all experience', and offers glimpses of 'that burning heart of life'. She felt that she could only produce poetry when she was 'possess[ed]', when her 'whole nature . . . suddenly leaped into life'. But she worried aloud to Gunn that her poems – 'about stars and mountains and light' – were too 'cold', too 'inhuman'. Still, she admitted, '[w]hen I'm possessed that's the only kind of thing that comes out of me.'

Four books in six years, and then – nothing. Shepherd would not publish another book for forty-three years. It's hard now to tell if her literary silence was down to discretion or to block. In 1931 – even at the apex of her output – she was smitten by something close to depression at her inability to write. 'I've gone dumb,' she wrote blackly to Gunn that year. 'One reaches (or I do) these dumb places in life. I suppose there's nothing for it but to go on living. Speech may come. Or it may not. And if it doesn't I suppose one has just to be content to be dumb. At least not shout for the mere sake of making a noise.' 'Speech' did come back to her after 1934, but only intermittently. She wrote little save for *The Living Mountain* – itself only about 30,000 words long – and the articles she contributed occasionally to the Deeside Field Club's journal.

Precise information about the composition of *The Living Mountain* is hard to come by. It was written mostly during the closing years of the Second World War, though it draws on Shepherd's lifetime of mountain experiences. War exists as distant thunder in the book: there are the aeroplanes that crash into the plateau, killing their crew; the blackout nights through which she walks to the one radio in the area to hear news of the campaigns; the felling of Scots pines on the Rothiemurchus estate for the war effort. We know that Shepherd had completed a draft by the late summer of 1945, because she sent a version to Gunn then for his scrutiny and opinion. 'Dear Nan, You don't need me to tell you how I enjoyed your book,' begins his astute reply:

This is beautifully done. With restraint, the fine precision of the artist or scientist or scholar; with an exactitude that is never pedantic but always tribute. So love comes

through, & wisdom . . . you deal with facts. And you
build with proposition, methodically and calmly, for light
and a state of being are facts in your world.

Gunn straightaway identifies the book's distinctive manners:
precision as a form of lyricism, attention as devotion, exactitude as tribute, description structured by proposition and facts
freed of their ballast such that they levitate and otherwise
behave curiously. But then his letter turns a little patronising.
He thinks that it will be 'difficult, perhaps' to get it published.
He suggests that she add photographs, and a map to help
readers for whom the 'proper nouns' of the Cairngorms will
mean nothing. He warns her away from Faber, who are in a
'mess', and suggests considering serial publication in *Scots
Magazine*. He congratulates her – his 'water sprite!' – on having
written something might interest 'hill & country lovers'.

Unable or unwilling to secure publication at the time, Shep-
herd placed the manuscript in a drawer for more than four
decades, until Aberdeen University Press finally and quietly
published it in 1977. That same year, Bruce Chatwin's *In
Patagonia*, Patrick Leigh Fermor's *A Time of Gifts* and John
McPhee's *Coming into the Country* appeared; a year later came
Peter Matthiessen's Zennish mountain epic, *The Snow Leopard*.
To my mind, *The Living Mountain* stands equal to these four
far better-known classics of place and travel. Along with J.A.
Baker's *The Peregrine* (1967) – with which it shares a compres-
sive intensity, a generic disobedience, a flaring prose-poetry
and an obsession (ocular, oracular) with the eyeball – it is
one of the two most remarkable twentieth-century British
studies of a landscape that I know. For many reasons – but

especially given the current surge of interest in 'nature writing' – it is a book that should find new generations of readers. I must be careful with the claims I make about it, for Shepherd despised blandishment. In a 1930 letter to Gunn she condemned 'the too too flattering ejaculations of the Scots press' who had reviewed her first two novels. 'Don't you loathe having your work over-praised?', she asked him. 'It makes me feel positively nasty towards the praiser.' I find it hard to imagine 'over-praising' this book, given how highly I regard it, but – the warning having been clearly issued – I will watch my step.

The Living Mountain is a formidably difficult book to describe. A celebratory prose-poem? A geo-poetic quest? A place-paean? A philosophical enquiry into the nature of knowledge? A metaphysical mash-up of Presbyterianism and the Tao? None of these descriptions quite fits the whole, though it is all of these things in part. Shepherd herself calls it 'a traffic of love', with 'traffic' implying 'exchange' and 'mutuality' rather than 'congestion' or 'blockage', and with a shudder of eroticism to that word 'love'. The language of the book is weathered in both senses: filled with different kinds of climate, but also the result of decades of contact with 'the elementals'. Tonally, it is characterised by the co-existence of 'clarity of the intellect' with 'surge[s] of emotion', and generically by the commingling of field-note, memoir, natural history and philosophical meditation. It is both exhilaratingly materialist – thrilled by the alterity of the Cairngorm granite, by a mountain-world which 'does nothing, absolutely nothing, but be itself' – and almost animist in its account of how mind and mountain interact.

Crucially, *The Living Mountain* needs to be understood as a parochial work in the most expansive sense. Over the past century, 'parochial' has soured as a word. The adjectival form of 'parish', it has come to connote sectarianism, insularity, boundedness: a mind or a community turned inward upon itself, a pejorative finitude. It hasn't always been this way, though. Patrick Kavanagh (1904–67), the great poet of the Irish mundane, was in no doubt as to the importance of the parish. For Kavanagh, the parish was not a perimeter but an aperture: a space through which the world could be seen. 'Parochialism is universal,' he wrote. 'It deals with the fundamentals.' Note that Kavanagh, like Aristotle, doesn't smudge the 'universal' into the 'general'. The 'general', for Aristotle, was the broad, the vague and the undiscerned. The 'universal', by contrast, consisted of fine-tuned principles, induced from an intense concentration on the particular. Again and again Kavanagh returned to this connection between the universal and the parochial, and to the idea that we learn by scrutiny of the close-at-hand. 'All great civilisations are based on parochialism,' he wrote finely:

> To know fully even one field or one land is a lifetime's experience. In the world of poetic experience it is depth that counts, not width. A gap in a hedge, a smooth rock surfacing a narrow lane, a view of a woody meadow, the stream at the junction of four small fields – these are as much as a man can fully experience.

Shepherd came to know the Cairngorms 'deeply' rather than 'widely', and they are to her what Selbourne was to Gilbert

White, the Sierra Nevada were to John Muir and the Aran Islands are to Tim Robinson. They were her inland-island, her personal parish, the area of territory that she loved, walked and studied over time such that concentration within its perimeters led to knowledge cubed rather than knowledge curbed. What, Shepherd once wondered to Gunn, if one could find a way to 'irradiate the common?' That, she concluded, 'should make something universal'. This irradiation of the 'common' into the 'universal' is what she achieved in *The Living Mountain*.

Most works of mountaineering literature have been written by men, and most male mountaineers are focussed on the summit: a mountain expedition being qualified by the success or failure of ascent. But to aim for the highest point is not the only way to climb a mountain, nor is a narrative of siege and assault the only way to write about one. Shepherd's book is best thought of, perhaps, not as a work of mountaineering literature but one of mountain literature. Early on, she confesses that as a young woman she had been prone to a 'lust' for 'the tang of height', and had approached the Cairngorms egocentrically, apprising them for their 'effect upon me'. She 'made always for the summits'. *The Living Mountain* relates how, over time, she learned to go into the hills aimlessly, 'merely to be with the mountain as one visits a friend, with no intention but to be with him'. 'I am on the plateau again, having gone round it like a dog in circles to see if it is a good place,' she begins one section, chattily. 'I think it is, and I am to stay up here for a while.' Circumambulation has replaced summit-fever; plateau has substituted for peak. She no longer has any interest in discovering a pinnacle-point from which she might become the *catascopos*, the looker-down who sees all with a god-like eye. Thus the brilliant image of the book's opening page (which has forever changed the way I perceive the Cairngorms) in which she proposes imagining the massif not as a series of individual summits, but instead as an entity: 'The plateau is the true summit of these mountains; they must be seen as a single mountain, and the individual tops . . . no more than eddies on the plateau surface.'

As a walker, then, Shepherd practises a kind of unpious pilgrimage. She tramps around, over, across and into the mountain, rather than charging up it. There is an implicit humility to her repeated acts of traverse, which stands as a corrective to the self-exaltation of the mountaineer's hunger for an utmost point. The pilgrim contents herself always with looking along and inwards to mystery, where the mountaineer longs to look down and outwards onto total knowledge.

The Cairngorms were my first mountain range, and they are still the hills I know best. My grandparents lived in a converted forestry cottage on a rare limestone upsurge on the north-eastern slopes of the massif, and the field of rough pasture which they owned ran down to the banks of the River Avon. From a young age, I visited them with my family, usually in the summers. On a wall of the house hung a vast laminated Ordnance Survey map of the whole range, on which we would finger-trace walks done and walks planned. My grandfather was a diplomat and mountaineer who had spent his life climbing around the world, and it was he and his Cairngorm world which cast the spell of height upon me as a child. His yard-long, wooden-hafted ice-axe and his old iron crampons seemed to my young imagination like the props of wizardry. I was shown black-and-white photographs of the peaks he had climbed in the Alps and the Himalayas, and it was miraculous to me that such structures could be ascended by humans. Mountaineering seemed to me then – as Shepherd puts it – 'a legendary task, which heroes, not men, accomplished'. And for me, as for Shepherd, childhood exposure to the Cairngorms 'thirled me for life to the mountain'. I have since crossed the massif on foot and ski many times, and my maps of the region are spidery with the marks of tracks followed and routes attempted. I have seen dozens of blue-white snow hares, big as dogs, popping up from behind peat hags over the back of Glas Maol, I have followed flocks of snow buntings as they gust over the Braeriach plateau, and I once spent hours sheltering in a snow-hole above the Northern Corries while a blizzard blew itself furiously out.

So I knew the Cairngorms long before I knew *The Living Mountain*, which I first read only in 2003, when it was recommended to me by a former friend. He spoke of it as a book that had almost slipped through the cracks of the canon; a lost classic. I read it, and was changed. I had thought that I knew the Cairngorms well, but Shepherd showed me my complacency. Her writing re-made my vision of these familiar hills. It taught me to see them, rather than just to look at them.

The Living Mountain is thick with the kinds of acute perception that come only from 'staying up for a while', from frequent crossings of a particular landscape. 'Birch needs rain to release its odour,' Shepherd notes. 'It is a scent with body to it, fruity like old brandy, and on a wet warm day one can be as good as drunk with it.' I had never before noticed the 'odour' of birches, but now cannot be in stand of birch trees on a rainy summer's day without smelling its Courvoisier whiff. Elsewhere Shepherd remarks and records 'the coil over coil' of a golden eagle's ascent on a thermal, 'the immature scarlet cups of the lichen', the flight of the 'white-winged ptarmigan', a pool of 'small frogs jumping like tiddly-winks', a white hare crossing sunlit snow with its accompanying 'odd ludicrous leggy shadow-skeleton'. She has an Andy Goldsworthy-ish eye for the inadvertent acts of land-art performed by the mountain: 'Beech bud-sheaths, blown in tide-mark lines along the edge of the roads, give a glow of brightness to the dusty roads of May.' She spends an October night in air that is 'bland as silk', and while half-asleep on the plutonic granite of the plateau feels herself become stone-like, 'rooted far down into immobility', meta-morphosed by the igneous rock into a newly mineral self.

Shepherd is a fierce see-er, then. And like many fierce see-ers, she is also a part-time mystic, for whom intense empir-icism is the first step to immanence. 'I knew when I had looked for a long time', she writes, 'that I had hardly begun to see.' Her descriptions often move beyond – or, rather, through – the material. Up on the mountain, she writes, after hours of walking and watching:

> the eye sees what it didn't see before, or sees in a new way what it had already seen. So the ear, the other senses. These moments come unpredictably, yet governed, it would seem, by a law whose working is dimly understood.

Shepherd – like Neil Gunn and like the Scottish explorer–

essayist W.H. Murray – was strongly influenced by her reading in Buddhism and the Tao. Shards of Zen philosophy glitter in the prose of all three writers, like mica flecks in granite. Reading their work now, with its fusion of Highland landscape and Buddhist metaphysics, remains astonishing: like encountering a Noh play performed in a kailyard, or chrysanthemums flourishing in a corrie.

'A mountain', says Shepherd Zennishly, 'has an inside.' This is what she calls her 'first idea', and it is a superbly counterintuitive proposition, for we tend to think of mountains in terms of their exteriors – peaks, shoulders, cliffs. But Shepherd is always looking *into* the Cairngorm landscape, and I now find myself doing the same when I am in the massif. Again and again her eyes pry through surfaces: into cracks in rocks, into the luminous interior of clear-watered lochs or rivers. She dips her hand into Loch Coire an Lochaine, she walks naked into the shallows of Loch Avon, she pokes fingers down mouse holes and into the snowpack. 'Into', in *The Living Mountain*, is a preposition that gains – by means of repeated use – the power of a verb. She goes to the mountain searching not for the great outdoors but for profound 'interiors', deep 'recesses'. The hidden volumes of landscapes fascinate her: the 'underground cavities' of the Ardennes, the 'hollows' and 'spectacular chasms' of the Cairngorms. The clarity of the water of the Grampian 'burns' and 'lochs' is so absolute that they appear to her 'like clear deeps of air, / Light massed upon itself'. Corries interest her for the ways in which they cup space and give 'body' and 'substance' to colour and to air. Writing of the eyes of creatures glimpsed in the 'dark of woodland' at dusk, she wonders if the green colour of their eyeballs

– the 'watergreen' – is the 'green of some strange void one sees . . . the glint of an outer light reflected or of an inner light unveiled'.

This preoccupation with the 'inside' of the mountain is no conceit; rather, it figures the book's attempts to achieve what she calls an 'accession of interiority'. For Shepherd, there was a continual traffic between the outer landscapes of the world and the inner landscapes of the spirit. She knew that topog raphy has long offered humans powerful allegories, keen ways of figuring ourselves to ourselves, strong means of shaping memories and giving form to thought. So it is that her book investigates the relationships that exist between the material and the metaphorical 'mountain'. She knew – as John Muir had written forty years earlier – that 'going out . . . was really going in'.

Partway through writing this essay, late in March, I left my home in Cambridge and travelled north to the Cairngorms on the sleeper train from London. In the south of England, black-thorn was foaming in the hedges, tulips and hyacinths were popping in suburban flower-beds, and spring was reaching full riot. Arriving in the Cairngorms, I found I had travelled back into high winter. Avalanches were still rumbling the lee slopes, Loch Avon was frozen over and blizzards were cruising the plateau. Over three days, with four friends, I crossed the massif on foot and ski from Glenshee in the south-east to Loch Morlich in the north-west. Up on the wide summit plateau of Ben a' Bhuird, I found myself in the purest 'white-out' condi-tions I have ever experienced. Those who have travelled in high mountains or to the poles are likely to be familiar with the white-out: the point at which snow, cloud and blizzard combine such that the world dissolves into a single pallor. Scale and distance become impossible to discern. There are no shadows or waymarks. Space is depthless. Even gravity's hold feels loosened: slope and fall-lines can only be inferred by the tilt of blood in the skull. It felt, for that astonishing hour up on Ben a' Bhuird, as if we were all flying in white space.

The mountain world, like the desert world, is filled with mirages: tricks of light and perspective, parhelia, fogbows, Brocken spectres, white-outs – illusions brought on by snow, mist, cloud or distance. These optical special-effects fascinated Shepherd. In winter, she sees a 'snow skeleton, attached to nothing', which turns out to be the black rocks of a cliff high above, whose apparent levitation is due to the imperceptibility of the snow banks below it. At midsummer, she looks through lucid air for hundreds of miles and spies an imaginary peak, a Hy Brasil of the high hills: 'I could have sworn I saw a shape, distinct and blue, very clear and small, further off than any hill the chart recorded. The chart was against me, my companions were against me, I never saw it again.' She punningly calls such illusions 'mis-spellings': visual 'errors' that possess an accidental magic and offer unlooked-for revelation. And she delights in these moments, rather than holding them in suspicion or correcting for them. For what she calls 'our gullible eyes', their proneness to 'deceptions' by the mountain world, are in fact a means of reconfiguring our reading of the world:

Such illusions, depending on how the eye is placed and used, drive home the truth that our habitual vision of things is not necessarily right: it is only one of an infinite number, and to glimpse an unfamiliar one, even for a moment, unmakes us, but steadies us again.

This is brilliantly seen and said. Our vision is never correct but only ever provisional. 'Illusions' are themselves means of knowing (a reminder of James Joyce's aside about errors being the portals of discovery). Importantly, these illusions cannot be summoned into being or ordered on request. They are unpredictable conspiracies of the material and the sensory; like the mountain as a whole, they are 'impossible to coerce'. Shepherd doesn't systematically traverse the mountain, or seek by some psychogeographic ruse to prise it open. She accepts that 'unheralded moment[s] of revelation' cannot be obtained 'at will'. The mountain is graceful in the Augustinian sense; its gifts cannot be actively sought (though mind you, there's more than a hint of good Deeside Presbyterianism in Shepherd's preoccupation with 'toil': 'On one toils, into the hill' . . . one encounters with relish 'a tough bit of going' . . . one 'toil[s] upward').

In one amazing passage about illusions, Shepherd describes looking from a distance at a stone barn on a humid day. The moist air acts as a lens, multiplying and redistributing her sightlines, so that she seems to view all sides of the barn simultaneously. Her own style possesses a similar dispersive quality. Reading *The Living Mountain*, your sight feels scattered – as though you've suddenly gained the compound eye of a dragonfly, seeing through a hundred different lenses at once. This multiplex effect is created by Shepherd's refusal to privilege a single perspective. Her own consciousness is only one among an infinite number of focal points on and in the mountain. Her prose watches now from the point of view of the eagle, now from that of the walker, now from that of the creeping juniper. In this way we are brought – in her memorable phrase – to see the earth 'as the earth must see itself'. This is a book which embodies ecological principles without being overtly 'environmental' (a word which would, I think, have meant little to Shepherd).

The first law of ecology is that everything is connected to everything else, and *The Living Mountain* is filled – woven – with images of weaving and interconnection. There are the pine roots that are 'twisted and intertwined like a cage of snakes'; the tiny Scots pines high on the hill that are 'splayed to the mountain and almost roseate in structure'; the duck and drake that, rising together, appear to form a single bird with 'two enormous wings'; the many-stranded lichen known locally as 'toadstails', with its dozens of 'separate trail[s] and side-branch[es]'; the loch currents which weave thousands of floating pine-needles into complex spheres, similar to wrens' nests: structures so intricately bound that 'they can be lifted out of the water and kept for years, a botanical puzzle to those who have not been told the secret of their formation' (these pine-needle balls are also, of course, surreptitious emblems of Shepherd's own tightly knit and tiny work, itself 'kept for years'). Reading through the book, you realise that its twelve sections are bound laterally to each other by rhymes of colour, thought and image, so that they offer not a dozen different facets of the mountain but rather a transverse descriptive weave – the prose equivalent of a dwarf juniper forest. In this way, the book's form acts out its central proposition, which is that the world will not fall into divisible realms, as an apple may be sliced, but is instead an unmappable mesh of interrelations.

In one scene Shepherd describes a long winter dusk spent watching two rutting stags, whose antlers have become 'interlaced' during a joust, such that they cannot separate. She sees them 'drag . . . each other backwards and forwards across the ringing frozen floor of a hollow', and waits for answers: who will win, how will they disentangle? But darkness falls, Shepherd is forced to return indoors, and even a return to the site of the battle the next morning yields neither corpses nor clues. The episode is yet another image of the mountain's refusal to answer to questions which are explicitly asked of it. That which 'interlocks' is rarely opened here, even by the 'keyed' senses of the walker. Deer run in a way that resembles flight, and yet their motion is 'fixed to the earth and cannot be detached from it'. A fawn lies in a 'hidden hollow', so camouflaged that its presence is given away only by the flick of its eyelid. The mountain 'does not come to an end with its rock and its soil', but has 'its own air'. Long before Lovelock gave us Gaia, Shepherd was proposing a holistic vision of her small world as one and indivisible: 'The disintegrating rock, the nurturing rain, the quickening sun, the seed, the root, the bird – all are one.' 'So there I lie on the plateau,' she writes:

> under me the central core of fire from which was thrust this grumbling grinding mass of plutonic rock, over me blue air, and between the fire of the rock and the fire of the sun, scree, soil and water, moss, grass, flower and tree,

insect, bird and beast, wind, rain and snow – the total mountain.

Shepherd's 'total' is of course totally distinct from the 'total' of 'totalising' or 'totalitarian'. Her mountain is 'total' insofar as it exceeds the possibility of our capacity ever to know it entirely.

It's for this reason that knowledge is never figured in *The Living Mountain* as finite: a goal to be reached or a state to be attained. The massif is not a crossword to be cracked, full of encrypted ups and downs. Man 'patiently adds fact to fact', but such epistemological bean-counting will only take you so far. No, knowledge is mystery's accomplice rather than its antagonist. Greater understanding of the mountain's inter-relations serves only to finesse the real into a further marvellousness, and to reveal other realms of incomprehension: 'The more one learns of this intricate interplay of soil, altitude, weather, and the living tissues of plant and insect . . . the more the mystery deepens.' Shepherd mentions her hydrological habit of following 'burns to their sources', but then remarks that the sources of the burns – the pools, the lochs, the lochans – hold further enigmas. The universe merely refers you onwards. Move along now. Keep on going. You'll encounter only new versions of 'that secret the mountain never quite gives away'.

What Shepherd learns – and what her book showed me – is that the true mark of long acquaintance with a single place is a readiness to accept uncertainty: a contentment with the knowledge that you must not seek complete knowledge. 'One never quite knows the mountain, nor oneself in relation

to it,' she writes. 'Knowing another is endless . . . The thing
to be known grows with the knowing.' 'Slowly I have found
my way in,' she says: slowly, but not fully, for '[i]f I had other
senses, there are other things I should know'. This is not a
book that relishes its own discoveries; it prefers to relish its
own ignorances – all those 'exciting properties of matter that
we cannot know because we have no way to know them', or
the water that is 'too much' for her, or the dark line of geese
that melts 'into the darkness of the cloud, and I could not
tell where or when they resumed formation and direction'.
Shepherd is compelled by the massif's excesses, its unmappable
surplus: 'The mind cannot carry away all that it has to give,
nor does it always believe possible what it has carried away.'

I worry that I may be making The Living Mountain sound
abstruse, cold, over-intellectual. It isn't, of course. It is deeply
wise and it is propositionally structured, but not abstruse. For
it's so full of life, death, body, gusto, touch and – subtly –
sexuality. To Shepherd, being on the mountain is a profoundly
physical experience. What joy she records! Up in the mountains, she lives off wild food, foraging for cranberries,
cloudberries and blueberries, drinking deeply from the 'strong
white' water of rivers. 'I am like a dog – smells excite me.
The earthy smell of moss . . . is best savoured by grubbing.'
She swims in lochs, and sleeps on hillsides to be woken by
the sharp click of a robin's foot upon her bare arm or the
snuffle of a grazing deer. She records with brilliant exactness
how frost 'stiffens the muscles of the chin' (a part of the body
we don't usually associate with muscularity, let alone thermo-
metric sensitivity), or the pleasure of 'running my hand after

rain through juniper . . . for the joy of the wet drops trickling over the palm'. Heather pollen rises from the moor which feels 'silky to the touch'. There is, unmistakably, an eroticism tingling through this book, *samizdat* and surreptitious, especially thrilling because Shepherd was a woman writing at a time and in a culture where candour about physical pleasure was widely regarded with suspicion. She relishes the touch of the world upon her thighs, calves, the soles of the feet, her hands. The body is made 'limber' by the rhythm of walking. 'Naked' recurs as a word – 'naked birch trees', 'naked' hands, 'naked legs'.

'That's the way to see the world: in our own bodies,' wrote the poet, Buddhist and forester Gary Snyder, and the phrase could stand as an epigraph to *The Living Mountain*. True, Shepherd knows well how rough mountains can be on the human body – sometimes fatally so. She admits to the 'roaring scourge' of the plateau in summer, when the midges are out in their millions and the heat rises in jellied waves from the granite; and she deplores the 'monstrous place' the mountain becomes when rain pours for hours on end. She describes getting burned by snow-glare until her eyes are weeping: she feels sick, and her face for days afterwards is left scorched 'as purple as a boozer's'. She demonstrates – like many mountain-goers – a macabre fascination with the dead of the hills: the five Czech airmen whose plane crashes into Ben a' Bhuird in low cloud; the five people dead by falling during the years Shepherd knows the hills; the four 'boys' who are caught and killed by storms, including the two who leave a 'high-spirited and happy report' in the waterproof log-book beneath the Shelter Stone at the west end of Loch Avon, but whose frozen bodies are later discovered on the hill, their knees and knuckles raw with abrasions from the granite boulders over which they had crawled, trying desperately to make their way in the blizzard wind.

For Shepherd, then, the body is at risk in the mountains – but it is also the site of reward, a fabulous sensorium. More than this: it is an auxiliary to the intellect. In the mountains, she writes, a life of the senses is lived so purely that 'the body may be said to think'. This is her book's most radical proposition. Radical because, as a philosophical position, it was cutting-edge. In the same years that Shepherd was writing *The Living Mountain*, the French philosopher Maurice Merleau-Ponty was developing his influential theories of the body-subject, as first laid out in his *The Phenomenology of Perception* (1945). Merleau-Ponty was at the time working as a professional philosopher in Paris with all the institutional support and vocational confidence that such a position brings. He had been trained as one of the French philosophical elite, studying alongside Sartre, de Beauvoir and Simone Weil at the École Normale Supérieure, where he passed the *agrégation* in philosophy in 1930. Shepherd was a teacher in an Aberdeen tertiary college, but her philosophical conclusions concerning colour-perception, touch and embodied knowledge now read as arrestingly similar to those of Merleau-Ponty.

For Merleau-Ponty, post-Cartesian philosophy had cleaved a false divide between the body and the mind. Throughout his career he argued for the foundational role that sensory perception plays in our understanding of the world as well in as our reception of it. He argued that knowledge is 'felt': that our bodies think and know in ways which precede cognition (the processing of experience by our minds). Consciousness, the human body and the phenomenal world are therefore inextricably intertwined or 'engaged'. The body 'incarnates' our subjectivity and we are thus, Merleau-Ponty proposed, 'embedded' in the 'flesh' of the world. He described this embodied experience as 'knowledge in the hands'; our body 'grips' the world for us and is 'our general medium for having a world'. And the world itself is therefore not the unchanging object presented by the natural sciences, but instead endlessly relational. It is made manifest only by presenting itself to a variety of views, and our perception of it is made possible by our bodies and their sensory-motor functions. We are co-natural with the world and it with us, but we only ever see it partially.

You'll already be able to hear the affinities between Merleau-Ponty's thought and Shepherd's, as well as between their dictions. On the mountain, she writes, moments occur at which 'something moves between me and it. Place and mind may interpenetrate until the nature of both are altered. I cannot tell what this movement is except by recounting it.' 'The body is not . . . negligible, but paramount,' she elsewhere declares, in a passage that could have come straight from *Phenomenology of Perception*. 'Flesh is not annihilated but fulfilled. One is not bodiless, but essential body':

> The hands have an infinity of pleasure in them. The feel of things, textures, surfaces, rough things like cones and bark, smooth things like stalks and feathers and pebbles rounded by water, the teasing of gossamers . . . the scratchiness of lichen, the warmth of the sun, the sting of hail, the blunt blow of tumbling water, the flow of wind

– nothing that I can touch or that touches me but has its own identity for the hand as much as for the eye.

Shepherd's belief in bodily thinking gives *The Living Mountain* a contemporary relevance. More and more of us live more and more separately from contact with nature. We have come increasingly to forget that our minds are shaped by the bodily experience of being in the world its spaces, textures, sounds, smells and habits – as well as by genetic traits we inherit and ideologies we absorb. We are literally losing touch, becoming disembodied, more than in any previous historical period. Shepherd saw this process starting over sixty years ago, and her book is both a mourning and a warning. One should use 'the whole of one's body to instruct the spirit', she wrote decisively to Gunn. 'This is the innocence we have lost,' she says, 'living in one sense at a time to live all the way through.' Her book is a hymn to 'living all the way through': to touching, tasting, smelling and hearing the world. If you manage this, then you might walk 'out of the body and into the mountain', such that you become, briefly, 'a stone . . . the soil of the earth'. And at that point then, well, then 'one has been in'. 'That is all', writes Shepherd, and that 'all' should be heard not diminutively, apologetically, but expansively, vastly.

Shepherd kept walking 'into' the Cairngorms until late in her long life. In her final months, however, harrowed by old age, she was confined to a nursing home near Banchory. She began to suffer illusions, 'confusions', mis-spellings. She hallucinated that the whole ward had been moved out to a wood in Drumoak: 'I can see the wood – I played in it as a child.' She began to see Grampian place-names blazoned in 'large capital letters' in a glowing arc across the 'dark and silent' room in which she slept. Even in this troubled state, Shepherd was still thinking hard about the nature of perception and about how to represent perception in language. 'It took old age to show me that time is a mode of experiencing,' she wrote to her friend, the Scottish artist Barbara Balmer, 'but how to convey such inwardness?' Reading true literature, she reflected, 'it's as though you are standing experiencing and suddenly the work is there, bursting out of its own ripeness . . . life has exploded, stick and rich and smelling oh so good. And . . . that makes the ordinary world magical – that rever-berates/illuminates.' This 'illumination' of the ordinary world was, of course, what Shepherd's own work achieved, though it would never have occurred to her to acknowledge her own exceptional power as a writer.

So the living mountain of Shepherd's title 'lives' because of our 'outgoing address' towards it. For her as for Merleau-Ponty, matter is 'impregnated with mind', and the world exists in a continuous 'active mood . . . the grammar of now, / The present tense'. Certain kinds of attention serve to 'widen the domain of being in the vastness of non-being'. Shepherd knows, of course, that this is largely delusory: that granite does not think, that corries do not sense our entry into 'their' space, and that rivers do not quench our thirst with pleasure or with resentment. She must not be mistaken for preaching either a superstitious animism or a lazy anthropomorphism ('I do not ascribe sentience to the mountain'). She offers, rather, a rigorous humanism, born of a phenomenology that

– astonishingly – she mostly deduced by walking rather than developed by reading.

For Shepherd, the body thinks best when the mind stops, when it is 'uncoupled' from the body. She writes exquisitely of those moments on the mountain when one is 'not bedeviled by thought'. 'They come to me most often,' she says, 'waking out of outdoor sleep, gazing tranced at the running of water and listening to its song.' But the best way of all to uncouple the mind is to walk: 'After hours of steady walking, with the long rhythm of motion sustained until motion is felt, not merely known by the brain, as the "still centre" of being . . . [you] walk the flesh transparent.' 'On the mountain', she says in the book's closing sentences, 'for an hour I am beyond desire. It is not ecstasy . . . I am not out of myself, but in myself. I am. That is the final grace accorded from the mountain.' This is Shepherd's revised version of Descartes' *cogito*. I walk therefore I am. The rhythm of the pedestrian, the iamb of the 'I am', the beat of the placed and lifted foot.

The more I read *The Living Mountain*, the more it gives to me. I have read it perhaps a dozen times now, and each time I re-approach it as Shepherd re-approaches the mountain; not expecting to exhaust it of its meaning, rather to be surprised by its fresh yields. New ways of seeing emerge, or at least I find myself shown how to look again from different angles. This book is tutelary, but it is not the expression of any system or program, spiritual or religious. There is no manifesto here, no message or neat take-home moral. As on the mountain, so in the book: the knowledge it offers arrives slantwise, from unexpected directions and quarters, and apparently limitlessly.

It is a book that grows with the knowing. 'However often I walk on them,' writes Shepherd of the Cairngorms, 'these hills hold astonishment for me . . . There is no getting accustomed to them.' However often I read *The Living Mountain*, it holds astonishment for me; there is no getting accustomed to it.

Cambridge–Cairngorms–Cambridge, 2011

Notes

The spelling of Scottish toponyms is a vexed business: the names of Cairngorm places given in this introduction and on the map are consistent with Nan Shepherd's usages in *The Living Mountain*. Warm thanks are due for various kinds of help in the writing of this introduction to Barbara Balmer, Janice Galloway, Naomi Geraghty, Grace Jackson, Hayden Lorimer, George Mackie and Roderick Watson. I am grateful to the Trustees of the National Library of Scotland and to Dairmid Gunn for permission to quote from unpublished letters. I have not supplied specific page references when quoting from *The Living Mountain*, so all unreferenced quotations should be assumed to have their origins in the book. Other sources for quoted material are given below.

'heaven-appointed task of trying': letter from Nan Shepherd to Neil Gunn, 2 April 1931, Deposit 209, Box 19, Folder 7, National Library of Scotland, Edinburgh.

'all movement, legs and arms': letter from Nan Shepherd to Barbara Balmer, 15 January 1981, private collection.

'library-cormorant': Samuel Taylor Coleridge, *Collected Letters, Vol I, 1785–1800*, ed. Earl Leslie Griggs (Oxford: Clarendon Press, 1966), p. 156.

'Poetry . . . in intensest being' through to 'burning heart of life': letter from Nan Shepherd to Neil Gunn, 14 March 1930, Deposit 209, Box 19, Folder 7, National Library of Scotland, Edinburgh.

'whole nature . . . suddenly leaped into life' through to 'the only kind of thing that comes out of me': letter from Nan Shepherd to Neil Gunn, 2 April 1931, Deposit 209, Box 19, Folder 7, National Library of Scotland, Edinburgh.

'I've gone dumb' through to 'making a noise': letter from Nan Shepherd to Neil Gunn, 2 April 1931, Deposit 209, Box 19, Folder 7, National Library of Scotland, Edinburgh.

'Dear Nan, You don't need me to tell you' through to 'facts in your world': letter from Neil Gunn to Nan Shepherd, 30 October 1945, Deposit 209, Box 19, Folder 7, National Library of Scotland, Edinburgh.

'difficult, perhaps' through to 'hill & country lovers': ibid.

'the too too flattering ejaculations' through to 'towards the praiser': letter from Nan Shepherd to Neil Gunn, 14 March 1930, Deposit 209, Box 19, Folder 7, National

Library of Scotland, Edinburgh.

'Parochialism is universal' through to 'as much as a man can fully experience': Patrick Kavanagh, 'The Parish and the Universe', in *Collected Pruse* [sic] (London: Macgibbon & Kee, 1967), pp. 281–83.

'irradiate the common?' through to 'make something universal': letter from Nan Shepherd to Neil Gunn, 2 April 1931, Deposit 209, Box 19, Folder 7, National Library of Scotland, Edinburgh.

'Beech bud-sheaths . . .': 'The Colour of Deeside', Nan Shepherd, *The Deeside Field*, 8 (Aberdeen: Aberdeen University Press, 1937), pp. 8–12; 9.

'like clear deeps of air': Nan Shepherd, 'The Hill Burns', loose poem, Deposit 209, Box 19, Folder 7, National Library of Scotland, Edinburgh.

'substance' through to 'an inner light unveiled': 'The Colour of Deeside', Nan Shepherd, *The Deeside Field*, 8 (Aberdeen: Aberdeen University Press, 1937), pp. 9–10.

'going out . . . was really going in': John Muir, journal entry, in *John of the Mountains: The Unpublished Journals of John Muir*, ed. L.M. Wolfe (Boston and New York: Houghton Mifflin Co, 1938), p. 427.

'gullible eyes': 'The Colour of Deeside', Nan Shepherd, *The Deeside Field*, 8 (Aberdeen: Aberdeen University Press, 1937), p. 11.

'That's the way to see the world': Gary Snyder, *The Practice of the Wild* (San Francisco: North Point Press, 1990), p. 106.

'incarnates' through to 'our general medium for having a world': Maurice Merleau-Ponty, *Phenomenology of Perception*, trans. Colin Smith (New York: Humanities Press, 1962), passim, but see especially pp. 144–46.

'the whole of one's body to instruct the spirit': letter from Nan Shepherd to Neil Gunn, May 1940, MS 26900, Deposit 209, Box 19, Folder 7, National Library of Scotland, Edinburgh.

'I can see the wood – I played in it as a child' through to 'that reverberates/illuminates': letters from Nan Shepherd to Barbara Balmer, 15 January and 2 February 1981, private collection.

'active mood . . . the grammar of now': Nan Shepherd, 'Achiltibuie', loose poem, Deposit 209, Box 19, Folder 7, National Library of Scotland, Edinburgh.

FOREWORD

Thirty years in the life of a mountain is nothing – the flicker of an eyelid. Yet in the thirty years since this book was written many things have happened to the Cairngorms, some of them spectacular things, things that have won them a place in the Press and on the television screens:

Aviemore erupts and goes on erupting.

Bulldozers *birse* their way into the hill.

Roads are made, and re-made, where there were never roads before.

Skiers, swift, elate, controlled, miracles of grace and precision, swoop and soar – or flounder – but all with exhilaration.

Chair-lifts swing up and swing down (and a small boy falls from one and is killed).

A restaurant hums on the heights and between it and the summit Cairn Gorm grows scruffy, the very heather tatty from the scrape of boots (too many boots, too much commotion, but then how much uplift for how many hearts). New shelters are sited for climbers. A cottage at Muir of Inverey is enlarged and fitted up as a place of resort for Cairngorm Club members, the members themselves laying the flooring and erecting the bunks.

Glenmore houses and trains those ready to learn. Skills are taught and tested. Young soldiers learn the techniques of Adventure. Orienteers spread over the land (but the Lairig Ghru, so far, is not to be tamed as part of a national 'way'). Reindeer are no longer experimental but settlers.

The Nature Conservancy provides safe covert for bird and beast and plant (but discourages vagabonds, of whom I have been shamelessly one – a peerer into corners). Ecologists investigate growth patterns and problems of erosion, and re-seed denuded slopes.

The Mountain Rescue service does its magnificent work, injured are plucked from ledges by helicopter, the located, the exhausted carried to safety.

And some are not rescued. A man and a girl are found, months too late, far out of their path, the girl on abraded hands and knees as she clawed her way through drift. I see her living face still (she was one of my students), a sane, eager, happy face. She should have lived to be old. Seventy men, with dogs and a helicopter, go out after a lone skier who has failed to return, and who is found dead. And a group of schoolchildren, belated, fail to find the hut where they should have spent the night. They shelter against a wall of snow, but in the morning, in spite of the heroic efforts of their instructress, only she and one boy are alive.

All these are matters that involve man. But behind them is the mountain itself, its substance, its strength, its structure, its weathers. It is fundamental to all that man does to it or on it. If it were not there he would not have done these things. So thirty years may alter the things he does but to know it in itself is still basic to his craft. And that is what, thirty years ago, I was striving to do in this manuscript. It was written during the latter years of the Second War and those just after. In that disturbed and uncertain world it was my secret place of ease. The only person who ever read the manuscript then was Neil Gunn, and that he should like it was not strange, because our minds met in just such experiences as I was striving to describe. He made a couple of suggestions as to publication, but added that in the circumstances of the time a publisher would be hard to find. I wrote one letter at his instigation and received a courteous and negative reply and the manuscript went into a drawer and has lain there ever since. Now, an old woman, I begin tidying out my possessions and reading it again I realise that the tale of my traffic with a mountain is as valid today as it was then. That it was a traffic of love is sufficiently clear; but love pursued with fervour is one of the roads to knowledge.

Nan Shepherd, August 1977

ONE

The Plateau

Summer on the high plateau can be delectable as honey; it can also be a roaring scourge. To those who love the place, both are good, since both are part of its essential nature. And it is to know its essential nature that I am seeking here. To know, that is, with the knowledge that is a process of living. This is not done easily nor in an hour. It is a tale too slow for the impatience of our age, not of immediate enough import for its desperate problems. Yet it has its own rare value. It is, for one thing, a corrective of glib assessment: one never quite knows the mountain, nor oneself in relation to it. However often I walk on them, these hills hold astonishment for me. There is no getting accustomed to them.

The Cairngorm Mountains are a mass of granite thrust up through the schists and gneiss that form the lower surrounding hills, planed down by the ice cap, and split, shattered and scooped by frost, glaciers and the strength of running water. Their physiognomy is in the geography books – so many square miles of area, so many lochs, so many summits of over 4000 feet – but this is a pallid simulacrum of their reality, which, like every reality that matters ultimately to human beings, is a reality of the mind.

The plateau is the true summit of these mountains; they must be seen as a single mountain, and the individual tops, Ben MacDhui, Braeriach and the rest, though sundered from one another by fissures and deep descents, are no more than eddies on the plateau surface. One does not look upwards to spectacular peaks but downwards from the peaks to spectacular chasms. The plateau itself is not spectacular. It is bare and very stony, and since there is nothing higher than itself (except for the tip of Ben Nevis) nearer than Norway, it is savaged by the wind. Snow covers it for half the year and sometimes, for as long as a month at a time, it is in cloud. Its growth is moss and lichen and sedge, and in June the clumps of Silene – moss campion – flower in brilliant pink. Dotterel and ptarmigan nest upon it, and springs ooze from its rock. By continental measurement its height is nothing much – around 4000 feet – but for an island it is well enough, and if the winds have unhindered range, so has the eye. It is island weather too, with no continent to steady it, and the place has as many aspects as there are gradations in the light.

Light in Scotland has a quality I have not met elsewhere. It is luminous without being fierce, penetrating to immense distances with an effortless intensity. So on a clear day one looks without any sense of strain from Morven in Caithness to the Lammermuirs, and out past Ben Nevis to Morar. At midsummer, I have had to be persuaded I was not seeing further even than that. I could have sworn I saw a shape, distinct and blue, very clear and small, further off than any hill the chart recorded. The chart was against me, my companions were against me, I never saw it again. On a day like that, height goes to one's head. Perhaps it was the lost Atlantis focused for a moment out of time.

The streams that fall over the edges of the plateau are clear – Avon indeed has become a by-word for clarity: gazing into its depths, one loses all sense of time, like the monk in the old story who listened to the blackbird.

> *Water of A'n, ye rin sae clear,*
> *'Twad beguile a man of a hundred year.*

Its waters are white, of a clearness so absolute that there is no image for them. Naked birches in April, lighted after heavy rain by the sun, might suggest their brilliance. Yet this is too sensational. The whiteness of these waters is simple. They are elemental transparency. Like roundness, or silence, their quality is natural, but is found so seldom in its absolute state that when we do so find it we are astonished.

The young Dee, as it flows out of the Garbh Choire and joins the water from the Lairig Pools, has the same astounding transparency. Water so clear cannot be imagined, but must be seen. One must go back, and back again, to look at it, for in the interval memory refuses to re-create its brightness. This is one of the reasons why the high plateau where these streams begin, the streams themselves, their cataracts and rocky beds, the corries, the whole wild enchantment, like a work of art is perpetually new when one returns to it. The mind cannot carry away all that it has to give, nor does it always believe possible what it has carried away.

So back one climbs, to the sources. Here the life of the rivers begins – Dee and Avon, the Derry, the Beinnie and the

Allt Druie. In these pure and terrible streams the rain, cloud and snow of the high Cairngorms are drained away. They rise from the granite, sun themselves a little on the unsheltered plateau and drop through air to their valleys. Or they cut their way out under wreaths of snow, escaping in a tumult. Or hang in tangles of ice on the rock faces. One cannot know the rivers till one has seen them at their sources; but this journey to the sources is not to be undertaken lightly. One walks among elementals, and elementals are not governable. There are awakened also in oneself by the contact elementals that are as unpredictable as wind or snow.

This may suggest that to reach the high plateau of the Cairngorms is difficult. But no, no such thing. Given clear air, and the unending daylight of a Northern summer, there is not one of the summits but can be reached by a moderately strong walker without distress. A strong walker will take a couple of summits. Circus walkers will plant flags on all six summits in a matter of fourteen hours. This may be fun, but is sterile. To pit oneself against the mountain is necessary for every climber: to pit oneself merely against other players, and make a race of it, is to reduce to the level of a game what is essentially an experience. Yet what a race-course for these boys to choose! To know the hills, and their own bodies, well enough to dare the exploit is their real achievement.

Mastering new routes up the rock itself is another matter. Granite, of which the Cairngorms are built, weathers too smoothly and squarely to make the best conditions for rock-climbing. Yet there is such challenge in the grandeur of the corries that those who climb cannot leave them untasted. The Guide Book and the *Cairngorm Club Journal* give the attested climbs, with their dates, from the end of last century onwards. Yet I wonder if young blood didn't attempt it sooner. There is a record of a shepherd, a century and a half ago, found frozen along with his sheep dog, on a ledge of one of the Braeriach cliffs. He, to be sure, wandered there, in a blizzard, but the men who brought down the body must have done a pretty job of work; and I can believe there were young hot-heads among that hardy breed to whom the scaling of a precipice was nothing new. Dr George Skene Keith, in his *General View of Aberdeenshire*, records having scrambled up the bed of the Dee cataract in 1810, and Professor McGil-livray, in his *Natural History of Braemar*, tells how as a student, in 1819, he walked from Aberdeen University to his western home, straight through the Cairngorm group; and lying down to sleep, just as he was, at the foot of the Braeriach precipices, continued next morning on his way straight up out of the corrie in which he had slept. On a later visit, searching out the flora of these mountains, he seems to have run up and down the crags with something of the deer's lightness. There are, however, ways up and down some of these corries that may be scrambled by any fleet-footed and level-headed climber, and it is doubtless these that the earlier adventurers had used. The fascination of the later work lies in finding ways impos-sible without the rope; and there are still many faces among these precipices that have not been attempted. One of my young friends lately pioneered a route out of the Garbh Choire of Braeriach, over rock not hitherto climbed. To him, one of the keenest young hillmen I know (he has been described, and recognised at a railway terminus, as 'a little black fellow, load the size of himself, with a far-away look in his eyes'), the mere setting up of a record is of very minor importance. What he values is a task that, demanding of him all he has and is, absorbs and so releases him entirely.

It is, of course, merely stupid to suppose that the record-breakers do not love the hills. Those who do not love them don't go up, and those who do can never have enough of it. It is an appetite that grows in feeding. Like drink and passion, it intensifies life to the point of glory. In the Scots term, used for the man who is *abune himsel'* with drink, one is *raised; fey;* a little mad, in the eyes of the folk who do not climb.

Fey may be too strong a term for that joyous release of body that is engendered by climbing; yet to the sober looker-on a man may seem to walk securely over dangerous places with the gay abandon that is said to be the mark of those who are doomed to death. How much of this gay security is the result of perfectly trained and co-ordinated body and mind, only climbers themselves realise; nor is there any need to ascribe to the agency of a god either the gay security, or the death which may occasionally, but rarely, follow. The latter, if it does occur, is likely to be the result of carelessness – of failing in one's exaltation to observe a coating of ice on the stone, of trusting to one's amazing luck rather than to one's compass, perhaps merely, in the glow of complete bodily well-being, of over-estimating one's powers of endurance.

But there is a phenomenon associated with this *feyness* of which I must confess a knowledge. Often, in my bed at home, I have remembered the places I have run lightly over with no sense of fear, and have gone cold to think of them. It seems to me then that I could never go back; my fear unmans me, horror is in my mouth. Yet when I go back, the same leap of the spirit carries me up. God or no god, I am *fey* again.

The *feyness* itself seems to me to have a physiological origin. Those who undergo it have the particular bodily make-up that functions at its most free and most live upon heights (although this, it is obvious, refers only to heights manageable to man and not at all to those for which a slow and painful acclimatisation is needful). As they ascend, the air grows rarer and more stimulating, the body feels lighter and they climb with less effort, till Dante's law of ascent on the Mount of Purgation seems to become a physical truth: 'This mountain is such, that ever at the beginning below 'tis toilsome, and the more a man ascends the less it wearies.'

At first I had thought that this lightness of body was a universal reaction to rarer air. It surprised me to discover that some people suffered malaise at altitudes that released me, but were happy in low valleys where I felt extinguished. Then I began to see that our devotions have more to do with our physiological peculiarities than we admit. I am a mountain lover because my body is at its best in the rarer air of the heights and communicates its elation to the mind. The obverse of this would seem to be exemplified in the extreme of fatigue I suffered while walking some two miles underground in the Ardennes caverns. This was plainly no case of a weary mind communicating its fatigue to the body, since I was enthralled by the strangeness and beauty of these underground cavities. Add to this eyes, the normal focus of which is for distance, and my delight in the expanse of space opened up from the mountain tops becomes also a perfect physiological adjustment. The short-sighted cannot love mountains as the long-sighted do. The sustained rhythm of movement in a long climb has also its part in inducing the sense of physical well-being, and this cannot be captured by any mechanical mode of ascent.

This bodily lightness, then, in the rarefied air, combines with the liberation of space to give mountain *feyness* to those who are susceptible to such a malady. For it is a malady, subverting the will and superseding the judgment: but a malady of which the afflicted will never ask to be cured. For this nonsense of physiology does not really explain it at all. What! am I such a slave that unless my flesh feels buoyant I cannot be free? No, there is more in the lust for a mountain top than a perfect physiological adjustment. What more there is lies within the mountain. Something moves between me and it. Place and a mind may interpenetrate till the nature of both is altered. I cannot tell what this movement is except by recounting it.

TWO

The Recesses

At first, mad to recover the tang of height, I made always for
the summits, and would not take time to explore the recesses.
But late one September I went on Braeriach with a man who
knew the hill better than I did then, and he took me aside
into Coire an Lochain. One could not have asked a fitter day
for the first vision of this rare loch. The equinoctial storms
had been severe; snow, that hardly ever fails to powder the
plateau about the third week of September, had fallen close
and thick, but now the storms had passed, the air was keen
and buoyant, with a brilliancy as of ice, the waters of the loch
were frost-cold to the fingers. And how still, how incredibly
withdrawn and tranquil. Climb as often as you will, Loch
Coire an Lochain remains incredible. It cannot be seen until
one stands almost on its lip, but only height hides it. Unlike
Avon and Etchachan, it is not shut into the mountain but
lies on an outer flank, its hollow ranged daily by all the eyes
that look at the Cairngorms from the Spey. Yet, without
knowing, one would not guess its presence and certainly not
its size. Two cataracts, the one that feeds it, falling from the
brim of the plateau over rock, and the one that drains it, show
as white threads on the mountain. Having scrambled up the

9

bed of the latter (not, as I knew later, the simple way, but my companion was a rabid naturalist who had business with every leaf, stalk and root in the rocky bed), one expects to be near the corrie, but no, it is still a long way off. And on one toils, into the hill. Black scatter of rock, pieces large as a house, pieces edged like a grater. A tough bit of going. And there at last is the loch, held tight back against the precipice. Yet as I turned, that September day, and looked back through the clear air, I could see straight out to ranges of distant hills. And that astonished me. To be so open and yet so secret! Its anonymity – Loch of the Corrie of the Loch, that is all – seems to guard this surprising secrecy. Other lochs, Avon, Morlich and the rest, have their distinctive names. One expects of them an idiosyncrasy. But Loch of the Corrie of the Loch, what could there be there? A tarn like any other. And then to find this distillation of loveliness!

I put my fingers in the water and found it cold. I listened to the waterfall until I no longer heard it. I let my eyes travel from shore to shore very slowly and was amazed at the width of the water. How could I have foreseen so large a loch, 3000-odd feet up, slipped away into this corrie which was only one of three upon one face of a mountain that was itself only a broken bit of the plateau? And a second time I let my eyes travel over the surface, slowly, from shore to shore, beginning at my feet and ending against the precipice. There is no way like that for savouring the extent of a water surface.

This changing of focus in the eye, moving the eye itself when looking at things that do not move, deepens one's sense of outer reality. Then static things may be caught in the very act of becoming. By so simple a matter, too, as altering the

position of one's head, a different kind of world may be made
to appear. Lay the head down, or better still, face away from
what you look at, and bend with straddled legs till you see
your world upside down. How new it has become! From the
close-by sprigs of heather to the most distant fold of the land,
each detail stands erect in its own validity. In no other way
have I seen of my own unaided sight that the earth is round.
As I watch, it arches its back, and each layer of landscape
bristles – though *bristles* is a word of too much commotion for
it. Details are no longer part of a grouping in a picture of
which I am the focal point, the focal point is everywhere.
Nothing has reference to me, the looker. This is how the earth
must see itself.

So I looked slowly across the Coire Loch, and began to
understand that haste can do nothing with these hills. I knew
when I had looked for a long time that I had hardly begun
to see. So with Loch Avon. My first encounter was sharp and
astringent, and has crystallised for ever for me some innermost
inaccessibility. I had climbed all six of the major summits,
some of them twice over, before clambering down into the
mountain trough that holds Loch Avon. This loch lies at an
altitude of some 2300 feet, but its banks soar up for another
fifteen hundred. Indeed farther, for Cairn Gorm and Ben
MacDhui may be said to be its banks. From the lower end of
this mile and a half gash in the rock, exit is easy but very
long. One may go down by the Avon itself, through ten miles
as lonely and unvisited as anything in the Cairngorms, to
Inchrory; or by easy enough watersheds pass into Strathnethy
or Glen Derry, or under the Barns of Bynack to the Caiplich
Water. But higher up the loch there is no way out, save by

scrambling up one or other of the burns that tumble from the heights: except that, above the Shelter Stone, a gap opens between the hills to Loch Etchachan, and here the scramble up is shorter.

The inner end of this gash has been howked straight from the granite. As one looks up from below, the agents would appear mere splashes of water, whose force might be turned aside by a pair of hands. Yet above the precipices we have found in one of these burns pools deep enough to bathe in. The water that pours over these grim bastions carries no sediment of any kind in its precipitate fall, which seems indeed to distil and aerate the water so that the loch far below is sparkling clear. This narrow loch has never, I believe, been sounded. I know its depth, though not in feet.

I first saw it on a cloudless day of early July. We had started at dawn, crossed Cairn Gorm about nine o'clock, and made our way by the Saddle to the lower end of the loch. Then we idled up the side, facing the gaunt corrie, and at last, when the noonday sun penetrated directly into the water, we stripped and bathed. The clear water was at our knees, then at our thighs. How clear it was only this walking into it could reveal. To look through it was to discover its own properties. What we saw under water had a sharper clarity than what we saw through air. We waded on into the brightness, and the width of the water increased, as it always does when one is on or in it, so that the loch no longer seemed narrow, but the far side was a long way off. Then I looked down; and at my feet there opened a gulf of brightness so profound that the mind stopped. We were standing on the edge of a shelf that ran some yards into the loch before plunging down to the pit that is the true bottom. And through that inordinate clearness we saw to the depth of the pit. So limpid was it that every stone was clear.

I motioned to my companion, who was a step behind, and she came, and glanced as I had down the submerged precipice. Then we looked into each other's eyes, and again into the pit. I waded slowly back into shallower water. There was nothing that seemed worth saying. My spirit was as naked as my body. It was one of the most defenceless moments of my life.

I do not think it was the imminence of personal bodily danger that shook me. I had not then, and have not in retrospect, any sense of having just escaped a deadly peril. I might of course have overbalanced and been drowned; but I do not think I would have stepped down unawares. Eye and foot acquire in rough walking a co-ordination that makes one distinctly aware of where the next step is to fall, even while watching sky and land. This watching, it is true, is of a general nature only; for attentive observation the body must be still. But in a general way, in country that is rough, but not difficult, one sees where one is and where one is going at the same time. I proved this sharply to myself one hot June day in Glen Quoich, when bounding down a slope of long heather towards the stream. With hardly a slackening of pace, eye detected and foot avoided a coiled adder on which the next spring would have landed me; detected and avoided also his mate, at full length in the line of my side spring; and I pulled up a short way past, to consider with amused surprise the speed and sureness of my own feet. Conscious thought had had small part in directing them.

So, although they say of the River Avon that men have

walked into it and been drowned, supposing it shallow because they could see its depth, I do not think I was in much danger just then of drowning, nor was fear the emotion with which I stared into the pool. That first glance down had shocked me to a heightened power of myself, in which even fear became a rare exhilaration: not that it ceased to be fear, but fear itself, so impersonal, so keenly apprehended, enlarged rather than constricted the spirit.

The inaccessibility of this loch is part of its power. Silence belongs to it. If jeeps find it out, or a funicular railway disfigures it, part of its meaning will be gone. The good of the greatest number is not here relevant. It is necessary to be sometimes exclusive, not on behalf of rank or wealth, but of those human qualities that can apprehend loneliness.

The presence of another person does not detract from, but enhances, the silence, if the other is the right sort of hill companion. (The perfect hill companion is the one whose identity is for the time being merged in that of the mountains, as you feel your own to be.) Then such speech as arises is part of a common life and cannot be alien. To 'make conversation', however, is ruinous, to speak may be superfluous. I have it from a gaunt elderly man, a 'lang tangle o' a chiel', with high cheek bones and hollow cheeks, product of a hill farm though himself a civil servant, that when he goes on the hill with chatterers, he 'could see them to an ill place'. I have walked myself with brilliant young people whose talk, entertaining, witty and incessant, yet left me weary and dispirited, because the hill did not speak. This does not imply that the only good talk on a hill is about the hill. All sorts of themes may be lit up from within by contact with it, as they are by contact with another mind, and so discussion may be salted. Yet to listen is better than to speak.

The talking tribe, I find, want sensation from the mountain – not in Keats's sense. Beginners, not unnaturally, do the same – I did myself. They want the startling view, the horrid pinnacle – sips of beer and tea instead of milk. Yet often the mountain gives itself most completely when I have no destination, when I reach nowhere in particular, but have gone out merely to be with the mountain as one visits a friend with no intention but to be with him.

THREE

The Group

My first climb was Ben MacDhui – rightly, since he is the highest – and by the classic route of Coire Etchachan; and from that first day two ideas persist. The first is that a mountain has an inside. I was well accustomed to hills, having run from child-hood on the Deeside hills and the Monadhliaths, those flowing heights that flank the Spey on the other side from the Cairn-gorms, an ideal playground for a child; and the end of a climb meant for me always the opening of a spacious view over the world: that was the moment of glory. But to toil upwards, feel the gradient slacken and the top approach, as one does at the end of the Etchachan ascent, and then find no spaciousness for reward, but an interior – that astounded me. And what an interior! the boulder-strewn plain, the silent shining loch, the black overhang of its precipice, the drop to Loch Avon and the soaring barricade of Cairn Gorm beyond, and on every side, except where we had entered, towering mountain walls.

Years later, I had something of the same sensation inside the Barns of Bynack, that enormous black cube of rock that lies like a Queen Anne mansion on the side of Ben Bynack. One can walk up a sort of staircase within and look out by a cleft as though from a window.

The second knowledge I have retained from my first ascent is of the inside of a cloud. For, from a few yards above Loch Etchachan to the summit, we walked in a cloud so thick that when the man who was leading went ahead by so much as an arm's length, he vanished, except for his whistle. His wife and I followed the whistle, and now and then when we were too slow (for he was an impatient lad), he materialised again out of the cloud and spoke to us. And alone in that whiteness, while our *revenant* came and went, we climbed an endless way. Nothing altered. Once, our ghostly mentor held us each firmly by an arm and said, 'That's Loch Etchachan down there.' Nothing. The whiteness was perhaps thicker. It was horrible to stand and stare into that pot of whiteness. The path went on. And now to the side of us there was a ghastlier white, spreading and swallowing even the grey-brown earth our minds had stood on. We had come to the snow. A white as of non-life.

That cloud, like others inside which I have walked, was wet but not wetting. It did not wet us till, almost at the summit, it broke in hard rain, and we could at last see the corries, scarfed in mist. Some clouds savage the wayfarer on the heights – clouds from below, up here they are rain, or sleet – some nuzzle him gently but with such persistence that he might as well walk through a loch. Or the wet may be more delicate, condensing in droplets on eyebrows and hair and woollen clothing, as has happened by morning with the dew after a night outside. Or the cloud may be hardly more than a sensation on the skin, clammy, or merely chill. Once I was inside a cloud that gave no sensation whatever. From within it, it was neither tangible nor visible, though as it approached it had looked thick and threatening. We were on the flank between Sgoran Dubh and Sgor Gaoith, on a cloudless day of sun; and suddenly there was the cloud, making steadily towards us, with a straight under-edge about the 3000 feet level. We thought: we're in for it! But nothing more happened than that the sunshine went out, as though a switch had clicked; and in some twenty minutes the sun clicked on again, and we saw the level under-edge of cloud pass away across the Einich valley. Inside the cloud had been just dry-dull.

To walk out through the top of a cloud is good. Once or twice I have had the luck to stand on a tip of ground and see a pearled and lustrous plain stretch out to the horizons. Far off, another peak lifts like a small island from the smother. It is like the morning of creation. Once, on Lochnagar, we had watched the dawn light strike the Cairngorms, like the blue bloom on plums. Each scarp and gully was translucent, no smallest detail blurred. A pure clear sun poured into each recess. But looking south, we caught our breath. For the world had vanished. There was nothing there but an immense stretch of hummocked snow. Or was it sea? It gleamed, and washed the high hills as the sea washes rock. And came to an end, as most seas do somewhere, with the Glen Lyon Mountains, Ben Lawers and Schiehallion, standing up out of it like one of the long twin-peaked islands of the west. A sea of mist invading the heart of the land, but sucked up by the sun as the hot day went on.

Seeing the Cairngorms from other mountains, Lochnagar or the Glen Lyon heights, emphasises them as a group. From the latter their great lift can be clearly seen, their mass and squareness. They tower up in a blunt pyramid. The height of high hills can, of course, be appreciated only from others of equal or at least approximate height, but this is not merely a matter of relative stature. There is something in their lift, their proportions and bearing, that can only be seen when one is somewhere near their own size. From below, oddly enough, they are not so majestic. This can be best seen with the Cairngorm group from Geal Charn in the Monadhliaths, which, though not even a three-thousander, stands erectly over against them across the Spey valley. Coming steeply down its front, one watches the high panorama opposite settle into itself as one descends. It enchants me like a juggler's trick. Every time I come down I want promptly to go back and see it all over again. A simple diagram explains the 'trick', but no diagram can explain the serene sublimity these high panoramas convey to the human mind. It is worth ascending unexciting heights if for nothing else than to see the big ones from nearer their own level.

From the hills of lower Deeside, the plateau nature of the group is most clearly seen, for only the long table of Ben Avon and Ben a' Bhuird is in view. As one follows up the Dee valley, Cairntoul appears, dominant. By Lochnagar, the whole façade is clear, sculptured in block and cleft and cornice, with which the light makes play. It is best at morning, when the cliffs are rose-red. The phenomenon lasts about an hour, precipice after precipice glowing to rose and fading again, though in some conditions of the air the glow lasts longer, and I have seen, in intense still summer heat, not only the corries but the whole plateau burning with a hot violet incandescence until noon. Sunset also lights the corries, but this must be seen on the other side of the group. From the Lochnagar side summer sunsets are behind the Cairngorms, but winter sunsets touch them obliquely. From Lochnagar, too, can be seen what is not often seen except by going to it or to those parts of the plateau just above it, one of the most secret places of the range, the inner recess of the great Garbh Choire of Braeriach.

On the hills still further west, from Glas Maol on the borders of Angus, the Cairngorm group seems to grow gently out of the surrounding hills, its outlines melting into harmony with theirs. Its origins may be different, but like them it has been subdued by the grinding of the Ice Age, and here more than anywhere else the common experience shows. From Ben Ouran at the head of Glen Ey, one looks straight into the Lairig Pass, and sees the plateau split in two by the cleft that runs right through it. But from the mouth of the Ey valley, on the hillside a mile or so from where this stream joins the Dee, one is surprised by a new vision of the familiar range. Here one realises: these are mountains, not a shattered plateau; for they are seen as peaks piled on peaks, a majestic culmination. This effect is most marked when the long flat top of Braeriach is veiled, as it is so often, in mist, while Ben MacDhui towers up like the giant he is, flanked by the peaked cone of Cairntoul and reinforced by the lesser and nearer peaks of the Devil's Point and Cairngorm of Derry. These peaks seem to hang splendidly aloft above the eye, giving a new sense of the grandeur of these mountains. But moving further round, south-west and west, one finds only a lump-mass, rounded and unshapely, with no dignity except bulk. This is the back of the mountain, like the back of a monster's head: at the other side are the open jaws, the teeth, the terrible fangs.

The north-east view, from the Braes of Abernethy, directly opposite to this lumpish back, has the gaping jaw and the fangs. It is a place of swift and soaring lines. This is Cairn Gorm, from which, though it is only the fourth summit in height, the whole group takes its name. These plunging precipices frame Loch Avon. Here is Stac Iolaire, the Eagle's Crag. Cairn Gorm has the finest complement of lochs – Loch Avon, the small and lovely Loch an Uaine, whose waters have the green gleam of old copper roofs, and Loch Morlich, the perfect mirror of the three great corries on the Speyside face. The edge of cliffs hangs 3000 feet above the smooth water, which is broad and long enough to hold the whole majestic front, corries, ridges and foothills, that jut like a high relief from the block of the plateau. On a still day it has a dream-like loveliness.

This whole north-west face, the three Cairn Gorm corries and the three on Braeriach, rises steeply from moor, so that walking along the plateau lip, one has the sense of being lifted, as on a mighty shelf, above the world.

FOUR

Water

So I am on the plateau again, having gone round it like a dog in circles to see if it is a good place. I think it is, and I am to stay up here for a while. I have left at dawn, and up here it is still morning. The midsummer sun has drawn up the moisture from the earth, so that for part of the way I walked in cloud, but now the last tendril has dissolved into the air and there is nothing in all the sky but light. I can see to the ends of the earth and far up into the sky.

As I stand there in the silence, I become aware that the silence is not complete. Water is speaking. I go towards it, and almost at once the view is lost: for the plateau has its own hollows, and this one slopes widely down to one of the great inward fissures, the Garbh Coire. It lies like a broad leaf veined with watercourses, that converge on the lip of the precipice to drop down in a cataract for 500 feet. This is the River Dee. Astonishingly, up here at 4000 feet, it is already a considerable stream. The immense leaf that it drains is bare, surfaced with stones, gravel, sometimes sand, and in places moss and grass grow on it. Here and there in the moss a few white stones have been piled together. I go to them, and water is welling up, strong and copious, pure cold water that flows away in rivulets and drops over the rock. These are the Wells of Dee. This is the river. Water, that strong white stuff, one of the four elemental mysteries, can here be seen at its origins. Like all profound mysteries, it is so simple that it frightens me. It wells from the rock, and flows away. For unnumbered years it has welled from the rock, and flowed away. It does nothing, absolutely nothing, but be itself.

The Dee, however, into which through its tributary streams all this south-eastern side of the Cairngorms is to drain, takes its headwaters not from one only but from both halves of the central plateau. The gash that divides the two halves (the Cairntoul and Braeriach from the Cairn Gorm-Ben MacDhui side), the Lairig Ghru, is so sheer and narrow that when mists roll among the precipices, lifting and settling again, it is sometimes hard to tell whether a glimpse of rock wall belongs to the mountain on which one is standing or to another across the cleft. High on the Ben MacDhui side, though 300 feet lower than the wells on Braeriach, two waters begin a mere step from one another. One runs east, falls over the precipice into Loch Avon and turns north to the Spey; the other, starting westwards, slips over the edge as the March Burn and falls into the Lairig Ghru. Eventually, turning south and east, and having joined the water that flows out of the Garbh Choire, it becomes the Dee. But where it falls into the narrow defile of the Lairig, its life seems already over. It disappears. A little further down a tiny pool is seen, and still further down two others, sizable pools, crystal clear and deep. They have no visible means of support, no stream is seen to enter them, none to leave; but their suppressed sparkle tells that they are living water. These are the Pools of Dee. The March Burn feeds them, the young Dee, a short way beyond the lowest of the pools, is plainly their exit. I can conceive of no good reason for trudging through the oppressive Lairig Ghru, except to see them.

Through most of its length the Lairig Ghru hides its watercourses. On the other side of the watershed, towards the Spey, this havoc of boulders seems quite dry. One is surprised when suddenly a piece of running stream appears in the bottom, but it is soon swallowed again. Finally, where the precipitous sides of the gash widen out, and the storms of centuries no longer have rained successions of broken boulders on to the stream beds, the burn at last gushes into the open, a full strong stream of crystal water.

It is not only in this narrow defile that the fallen and scattered boulders cover the watercourses. I have sat among boulders on an outer face of the hill, with two low sounds in my ears, and failed to locate either. One was the churr of ptarmigan, the other the running of water. After a long time, I saw the ptarmigan when he rose with a movement of white wings from among the grey stones he so closely resembles, but the water I never saw. In other places a bottle-neck gurgle catches my ear and where I thought there were only stones, I can see below them the glint of water.

The Cairngorm water is all clear. Flowing from granite, with no peat to darken it, it has never the golden amber, the 'horse-back brown' so often praised in Highland burns. When it has any colour at all, it is green, as in the Quoich near its linn. It is a green like the green of winter skies, but lucent, clear like aquamarines, without the vivid brilliance of glacier water. Sometimes the Quoich waterfalls have violet playing through the green, and the pouring water spouts and bubbles in a violet froth. The pools beneath these waterfalls are clear and deep. I have played myself often by pitching into them the tiniest white stones I can find, and watching through the appreciable time they take to sway downwards to the bottom.

Some of the lochs also are green. Four of them bear this quality in their names – Loch an Uaine. They are all small lochs, set high in corries, except for the Ryvoan Loch, the lowest and most decorative. Perhaps I should say, decorated. It lies within the tree level, which none of the others do, and has a lovely frieze of pine trees, an eagle's eyrie in one of them, and ancient fallen trunks visible at its bottom through the clear water. The greenness of the water varies according to the light, now aquamarine, now verdigris, but it is always pure green, metallic rather than vegetable. That one which hangs between a precipice and sloping slabs of naked rock on the face of the great curve of cliffs between Braeriach and Cairntoul has the sharpest beauty of the four – a stark splendour of line etched and impeccable. Ben MacDhui and Cairngorm of Derry have the other two, less picturesque than the first, less exquisite than the other. The Spey slope of these mountains has the best of it with lochs, but the Dee slope has the lovelier burns – they fall more steeply, with deep still pools below the falls.

Two of the lochs are black by name – the Dubh Loch of Ben a' Bhuird, and the Dubh Loch that lies in the second cleft that cuts the plateau, the Little Lairig; but they are black by place and not by nature, shadowed heavily by rock. That the water has no darkness in it is plain when one remembers that the clear green Quoich runs out of the one loch and the

Avon is fed by the other. In winter the ice that covers them has green glints in it, and in April dark streaks run through the glinting ice, showing where the springs are already running strong beneath. In summer I have stood on the high buttress of Ben a' Bhuird above the Dubh Loch, with the sun striking straight downwards into its water, and seen from that height through the water the stones upon its floor.

This water from the granite is cold. To drink it at the source makes the throat tingle. A sting of life is in its touch. Yet there are midsummer days when even on the plateau the streams are warm enough to bathe in. In other years on the same date the same streams surge out from caves of snow, and snow bridges span not only the Dee on its high plateau but the Etchachan in its low hung corrie; and fording the Allt Druie, which is too swollen to cross dryshod, I have been aware of no sensation at all, not even of the pressure of the current against my legs, but cold.

The sound of all this moving water is as integral to the mountain as pollen to the flower. One hears it without listening as one breathes without thinking. But to a listening ear the sound disintegrates into many different notes – the slow slap of a loch, the high clear trill of a rivulet, the roar of spate. On one short stretch of burn the ear may distinguish a dozen different notes at once.

When the snows melt, when a cloud bursts, or rain teems out of the sky for days on end without intermission, then the burns come down in spate. The narrow channels cannot contain the water, which streams down the hillsides, tears deep grooves in the soil, rolls the boulders about, brawls, obliterates paths, floods burrows, swamps nests, uproots trees, and finally reaching the more level ground, becomes a moving sea. Roads that were mended after the last spate are stripped to their bones, bridges are washed away. My path comes to a place where I had forgotten there was a bridge – it is a mere plank over a ditch. The plank hasn't been moved, but now it lies deep under a roaring race of water twenty feet wide. I try to ford it, and almost at once the water is mid-way between knee and thigh, and my body is tensed with the effort to stand erect against its sweep. I step cautiously forward not lifting my feet, sliding them along the bottom as an old gamekeeper has taught me, but before I reach the middle I am afraid. I retreat. There is another way round.

But sometimes there may not be another way round. Standing there with the racing water against my thigh, I understand why, in days when there were few bridges and the ill-made (or un-made) roads went by the fordable places, so many Scottish streams had a sinister reputation. Avon had an ill name for drownings, like Till of the old rhyme. Even within my lifetime, both Spey and Dee have had many victims.

For the most appalling quality of water is its strength. I love its flash and gleam, its music, its pliancy and grace, its slap against my body; but I fear its strength. I fear it as my ancestors must have feared the natural forces that they worshipped. All the mysteries are in its movement. It slips out of holes in the earth like the ancient snake. I have seen its birth; and the more I gaze at that sure and unremitting surge of water at the very top of the mountain, the more I am baffled. We make it all so easy, any child in school can understand it – water rises in the hills, it flows and finds its own level, and man can't live without it. But I don't understand it. I cannot fathom its power.

When I was a child, I loved to hold my fingers over the tap at full cock and press with all my puny strength until the water defeated me and spurted over my newly-laundered frock. Sometimes I have had an insane impulse to hold back with my fingers a mountain spring. Absurd and futile gesture! The water is too much for me. I only know that man can't live without it. He must see it and hear it, touch and taste it, and, no, not smell it, if he is to be in health.

FIVE

Frost and Snow

The freezing of running water is another mystery. The strong white stuff, whose power I have felt in swollen streams, which I have watched pour over ledges in endless ease, is itself held and punished. But the struggle between frost and the force in running water is not quickly over. The battle fluctuates, and at the point of fluctuation between the motion in water and the immobility of frost, strange and beautiful forms are evolved. Until I spent a whole midwinter day wandering from one burn to another watching them, I had no idea how many fantastic shapes the freezing of running water took. In each whorl and spike one catches the moment of equilibrium between two elemental forces.

The first time I really looked at this shaping process was in the Slugain valley on a January day. The temperature in Braemar village had fallen the previous night to – 2°F. We had climbed Morrone in the afternoon, and seen sunset and the rise of a full moon together over a world that was completely white except for some clumps of firwood that looked completely black. (In Glen Quoich next day the ancient fir trees far up the valley had the same dead black look – no green in them at all.) The intense frost, the cloudless sky, the white world, the setting sun and the rising moon, as we gazed on them from the slope of Morrone, melted into a prismatic radiation of blue, helio, mauve, and rose. The full moon floated up into green light; and as the rose and violet hues spread over snow and sky, the colour seemed to live its own life, to have body and resilience, as though we were not looking at it, but were inside its substance.

Next day a brilliant sun spangled the snow and the precipices of Ben a' Bhuird hung bright rose-red above us. How crisp, how bright a world! but, except for the crunch of our own boots on the snow, how silent. Once some grouse fled noiselessly away and we lifted our heads quickly to look for a hunting eagle. And down valley he came, sailing so low above our heads that we could see the separate feathers of the pinions against the sky, and the lovely lift of the wings when he steadied them to soar. Near the top of the glen there were coal-tits in a tree, and once a dipper plunged outright into the icy stream. But it was not an empty world. For everywhere in the snow were the tracks of birds and animals.

The animals had fared as we did: sometimes we stepped buoyantly over the surface of drifts, sometimes sank in well above the knees. Sometimes the tracks were deep holes in the snow, impossible to read except by the pattern in which they were placed; sometimes the mark of the pad was clear, just sunk into the snow surface, and at other times only four, or five, spaced pricks showed where the claws had pierced.

These tracks give to winter hill walking a distinctive pleasure. One is companioned, though not in time. A hare bounding, a hare trotting, a fox dragging his brush, grouse thick-footed, plover thin, red deer and roes have passed this way. In paw depressions may be a delicate tracery of frost. Or a hare's tracks may stand up in ice-relief above the softer snow that has been blown from around them. In soft dry snow the pad of a hare makes a leaflike pattern. A tiny track, like twin beads on a slender thread, appears suddenly in the middle of virgin snow. An exploring finger finds a tunnel in the snow, from which the small mouse must have emerged.

But while birds and tracks (we saw nothing four-footed that morning) amused us as we went up the Slugain, our most exquisite entertainment came from the water. Since then I have watched many burns in the process of freezing, but I do not know if description can describe these delicate manifestations. Each is an interplay between two movements in simultaneous action, the freezing of frost and the running of water. Sometimes a third force, the blowing of wind, complicates the forms still further. The ice may be crystal clear, but more probably is translucent; crimpled, crackled or bubbled; green throughout or at the edges. Where the water comes wreathing over stones the ice is opaque, in broken circular structure. Where the water runs thinly over a line of stones right across the bed and freezes in crinkled green cascades of ice, then a dam forms further up of half frozen slush, green, though colourless if lifted out, solid at its margins, foliated, with the edges all separate, like untrimmed hand-made paper, and each edge a vivid green. Where water drips steadily from an overhang, undeflected by wind, almost perfect spheres of clear transparent ice result. They look unreal, in this world of wayward undulations, too regular, as though man had made them. Spray splashing off a stone cuts into the slowly freezing snow on the bank and flutes it with crystal, or drenches a sprig of heather that hardens to a tree of purest glass, like an ingenious toy. Water running over a rock face freezes in ropes, with the ply visible. Where the water fell clear of the rock icicles hang, thick as a thigh, many feet in length, and sometimes when the wind blows the falling water askew as it freezes, the icicles are squint. I have seen icicles like a scimitar blade in shape, firm and solid in their place. For once, even the wind has been fixed. Sometimes a smooth portion of stream is covered with a thin coat of ice that, not quite meeting in the middle, shows the level of the water several inches below; since the freezing began, the water upstream has frozen and less water is flowing. When a level surface has frozen hard from bank to bank, one may hear at times a loud knocking, as the stream, rushing below the ice, flings a stone up against its roof. In boggy parts by the burnside one treads on what seems solid frozen snow, to find only a thin crisp crust that gives way to reveal massed thousands of needle crystals of ice, fluted columns four or five inches deep. And if one can look below the covering ice on a frozen burn, a lovely pattern of fluted indentations is found, arched and chiselled, the obverse of the water's surface, with the subtle shift of emphasis and superimposed design that occurs between a painting and the landscape it represents. In short, there is no end to the lovely things that frost and the running of water can create between them.

When the ice-paws crisped round the stones in the burns, and the ice-carrots that hang from the ledges, are loosened, and the freed ice floats down the river, it looks like masses of floating water lilies, or bunching cauliflower heads. Sunset plays through this greenish-white mass in iridescent gleams. At one point (I have heard of it nowhere else) near the exit of a loch, the peculiar motion of the current among ice-floes has woven the thousands of floating pine-needles into compacted balls, so intricately intertwined that their symmetrical shape is permanently retained. They can be lifted out of the water and kept for years, a botanical puzzle to those who have not been told the secret of their formation.

Snow too can be played with by frost and wind. Loose snow blown in the sun looks like the ripples running through corn. Small snow on a furious gale freezes on the sheltered side of stones on a hilltop in long crystals; I have seen these converge slightly as the wind blows round both sides of the stones. Another fixation of the wind. Or the wind lifts the surface of loose snow but before it has detached it from the rest of the snow, frost has petrified the delicate shavings in flounces of transparent muslin. 'Prince of Wales Feathers', one of my friends has called a similar materialisation of wind and frost. Snow can blow past in a cloud, visible as it approaches, but formed of minute ice particles, so fine that the eye cannot distinguish them individually as they pass. Set the hand against them and it is covered by infinitesimal droplets of water whose impact has hardly been felt, though if the face is turned towards them, the spicules sting the eyeball. Such snow lies in a ghostly thin powdering on the hillside, like the 'glaister o' sifted snaw' that fell on the head of the old Scots minister in his ill-roofed kirk.

The coming of snow is often from a sky of glittering blue, with serried battalions of solid white cumuli low on the horizon. One of them bellies out from the ranks, and from its edge thin shreds of snow, so fine one is hardly aware of their presence, eddy lightly in the blue sky. And in a few minutes the air is thick with flakes. Once the snow has fallen, and the gullies are choked and ice is in the burns, green is the most characteristic colour in sky and water. Burns and river alike have a green glint when seen between snowy banks, and the smoke from a woodman's fire looks greenish against the snow. The shadows on snow are of course blue, but where snow is blown into ripples, the shadowed undercut portion can look quite green. A snowy sky is often pure green, not only at sunrise or sunset, but all day; and a snow-green sky looks greener in reflection, either in water or from windows, than it seems in reality. Against such a sky, a snow-covered hill may look purplish, as though washed in blaeberry. On the other hand, before a fresh snowfall, whole lengths of snowy hill may appear a golden green. One small hill stands out from this greenness: it is veiled by a wide-spaced fringe of fir trees, and behind them the whole snowy surface of the hill is burning with a vivid electric blue.

The appearance of the whole group, seen from without, while snow is taking possession, changes with every air. A thin covering of snow, through which the rock structure breaks, can look more insubstantial than the most diaphanous blue – a phantom created from reality. When the snow is melting, and the plateau is still white but the lower slopes are streaked and patched, against a grey-white sky only the dark portions show; the plateau isn't there, the ridges that run up to the corries stand out like pinnacles and aiguilles. Later, at evening, the sky has turned a deep slate blue, identical with the blue that now washes the bare lower stretches of the mountains, and the long high level summit of snow, with its downward-reaching tentacles, hangs unsupported.

When the mountains are at last completely covered in with snow (and it doesn't happen every winter, so unpredictable is this Cairngorm weather – the skiers may wait far into the spring in vain for the right depth and surface of snow), then on a sunny day the scintillation is bright but does not wound. The winter light has not the strength to harm. I have never myself found it distressing to the eyes, though sometimes I have walked all day through millions of sparkling sun spangles on the frosty snow. The only time I have suffered from snow-blindness was at the very end of April, by which time, five or six weeks after the equinox, this northern light has become strong. I have heard of a strange delusion that the sun does not shine up here. It does; and because of the clarity of the air its light has power: it has more power, I suppose, in light than in heat. On that late April day, after some halcyon weather, a sudden snow storm blew up. It snowed all night – thick heavy snow that lay even under the next day's sunshine. We were going to the Dubh Loch of Ben a' Bhuird, with no intention of a summit, and I had taken no precautions against exposure; I had expected neither frosty wind nor hot sun to play havoc with my skin, nor had I had till then any experience of strong light upon snow. After a while I found the glare intolerable; I saw scarlet patches on the snow; I felt sick and weak. My companion refused to leave me sitting in the snow and I refused to defeat the object of his walk, which was to photograph the loch in its still wintry condition; so I struggled on, with his dark handkerchief veiling my eyes – a miserable blinkered imprisonment – and in time we were shadowed by the dark sides of the corrie. I was badly burned that day too; for some days my face was as purple as a boozer's; all of which discomfort I might have avoided had I remembered that snow can blow out of a warm sky.

It is not, however, such freak storms that are of moment, but the January blizzards, thick, close and wild – the *blin' drift* that shuts a man into deadly isolation. To go into such conditions on the mountain is folly; the gamekeeper's dictum is: if you can't see your own footsteps behind you in the snow, don't go on. But a blizzard may blow up so rapidly that one is caught. The great storms, when the snow beats down thick and solid for days on end, piling into the bowls of the corries, pressing itself down by its own weight, may be seen gathering over the mountains before they spread and cover the rest of the earth. I watched the preparation of the storm that was called, when it broke upon the country, the worst for over fifty years. I watched, from the shoulder of Morrone, the Cairngorm mass eddy and sink and rise (as it seemed) like a tossed wreck on a yellow sea. Sky and the wrack of precipice and overhang were confounded together. Now a spar, now a mast, just recognisable as buttress or cornice, tossed for a moment in the boiling sea of cloud. Then the sea closed on it, to open again with another glimpse of mounting spars – a shape drove its way for a moment through the smother, and was drawn under by the vicious swirl. Ashen and yellow, the sky kicked convulsively.

All this while the earth around me was bare. Throughout December the ground had been continuously white, but in the first week of the year there came a day like April, the snow sunned itself away and the land basked mildly in the soft airs. But now the commotion among the mountains lashed out in whips of wind that reached me where I stood watching. Soon I could hardly stand erect against their force. And on the wind sailed minute thistledowns of snow, mere gossamers. Their fragility, insubstantial almost as air, presaged a weight and solidity of snow that was to lie on the land for many weeks.

In the corries the tight-packed snow stands for many months. Indeed, until a succession of unusually hot summers from 1932 to 1934, even in July there were solid walls of snow, many feet thick and as high as the corrie precipices, leaning outwards from the rock and following its contours. There was snow worth seeing in those old summers. I used to believe it was enternal snow, and touched it with a feeling of awe. But by August 1934, there was no snow left at all in the Cairngorms except a small patch in the innermost recess of the Garbh Choire of Braeriach. Antiquity has gone from our snow.

It was in the storm whose beginnings I have described, during a blizzard, that a plane containing five Czech airmen crashed into Ben a' Bhuird. That its impact was made in deep snow was clear from the condition of the engines, which were only a little damaged.

Blizzard is the most deadly condition of these hills. It is wind that is to be feared, even more than snow itself. Of the lives that have been lost in the Cairngorms while I have been frequenting them (there have been about a dozen, excepting those who have perished in plane crashes) four were lost in blizzard. Three fell from the rock – one of these a girl. One was betrayed by the ice-hard condition of a patch of snow in

May, and slipped. All these were young. Two older men have gone out, and disappeared. The body of one of these was discovered two years later.

Of the four who were caught in blizzard, two died on 2 January 1928, and two on the same date in 1933. The former two spent their last night in the then disused cottage where I have since passed some of the happiest times of my life. Old Sandy Mackenzie the stalker, still alive then, in the other small house on the croft, warned the boys against the blizzard. As I sit with Mrs Mackenzie, now, by the open fireplace, with a gale howling in the chimney and rattling the iron roof ('this tin-can of a place', she calls it), and watch her wrinkled hands build the fir-roots for a blaze, she tells me of the wind that was in it. I listen to the smashing of this later gale, which has blown all night. 'If you had been getting up and going away the house would have been following you,' she says, knowing my habit of sleeping by the door and prowling at all sorts of hours. And remembering how I crept down into my bag last night, I picture those two boys lying on the floor in the empty house, with the roof rattling and the icy wind finding every chink. Not that they had cared. They asked for nothing but a roof. 'And salt – they asked for salt.' Strange symbolic need of a couple of boys who were to find no hospitality again on earth. Her old bleared eyes look into the distance. She says, 'the snow would be freezing before it would be on your cheek.' John, the son, found the second body in March, in a snow drift that he and his West Highland terrier had passed many times. 'But that morning,' he told me, 'she was scraping.' 'You will not be finding a thing but in the place where it will be', says the old woman. She had fetched the bellows and blown the logs into a flame. 'Sandy used to say, *The fire is the finest flower of them all*, when he would be coming in from the hill.' She makes the tea. But she has brought the storm in to our fireside, and it stays there through the night.

The other two boys went over Cairn Gorm in the kind of miraculous midwinter weather that sometimes occurs, and slept the night at the Shelter Stone beside Loch Avon. They were local boys. In the July of that year, on a very fine Sunday when we had gone out at dawn and had an empty hill all morning to ourselves, we saw with amazement a stream of people come up the hill the easy way from Glenmore and pass over and down to the Shelter Stone. We counted a hundred persons on the hill. They had come to see the place where the two boys slept and to read their high-spirited and happy report in the book that lies in its waterproof cover beneath the huge balanced boulder that has sheltered so many sleepers. That they would not reach home when they set out that morning after writing it, they could not dream. One of them was an experienced hill walker. But they reckoned without the wind. The schoolmistress of the tiny school at Dorback, which lies under Cairn Gorm on the Abernethy side, told me, of that wind, that her crippled sister, crossing the open space of the playground, was blown from her feet. And five miles from Glenmore and safety, crawling down Coire Cas on hands and knees, the boys could fight the wind no further. It was days later till they found them; and one of the men who was at the finding described to me their abraded knees and knuckles. The elder of the two was still crawling, on hands and knees, when they found him fast in the drift. *So quick bright things come to confusion.* They committed, I suppose, an error of judgment, but I cannot judge them. For it is the risk we must all take when we accept individual responsibility for ourselves on the mountain, and until we have done that, we do not begin to know it.

SIX

Air and Light

In the rarefied air of the plateau, and indeed anywhere in the
mountain, for the air is clear everywhere, shadows are sharp
and intense. Watch the shadow of a plane glide along the
plateau like a solid thing, and then slither deformed over the
edge. Or pluck a feathery grass, brownish-pink and inconspicuous; hold a sheet of white paper behind it and see how
the shadow stands out like an etching, distinct and black, a
miracle of exact detail. Even the delicate fringe inside the
small cup of the field gentian throws its shadow on the petals
and enhances their beauty.

The air is part of the mountain, which does not come to
an end with its rock and its soil. It has its own air; and it is
to the quality of its air that is due the endless diversity of its
colourings. Brown for the most part in themselves, as soon as
we see them clothed in air the hills become blue. Every shade
of blue, from opalescent milky-white to indigo, is there. They
are most opulently blue when rain is in the air. Then the
gullies are violet. Gentian and delphinium hues, with fire in
them, lurk in the folds.

These sultry blues have more emotional effect than a dry

air can produce. One is not moved by china blue. But the violet range of colours can trouble the mind like music. Moisture in the air is also the cause of those shifts in the apparent size, remoteness, and height in the sky of familiar hills. This is part of the horror of walking in mist on the plateau, for suddenly through a gap one sees solid ground that seems three steps away, but lies in sober fact beyond a 2000 foot chasm. I stood once on a hill staring at an opposite hill that had thrust its face into mine. I stared until, dropping my eyes, I saw with astonishment between me and it a loch that I knew perfectly well was there. But it couldn't be. There wasn't room. I looked up again at that out-thrust brow – it was so near I could have touched it. And when I looked down, the loch was still there. And once in the Monadhliaths, on a soft spring day when the distances were hazed, valley, hills and sky all being a faintly luminous grey-blue, with no detail, I was suddenly aware of a pattern of definite white lines high above me in the sky. The pattern defined itself more clearly; it was familiar; I realised it was the pattern of the plateau edge and corries of the Cairngorms, where the unmelted snow still lay. There it hung, a snow skeleton, attached to nothing, much higher than I should have expected it to be. Perhaps the lack of detail in the intervening valley had something to do with this effect.

Rain in the air has also the odd power of letting one see things in the round, as though stereoscopically. The rays of light, refracted through the moisture in the air, bend round the back of what I am seeing. I have looked at a croft half a mile away lying into the hill, with a steading and a cow, and felt as though I were walking round the stacks and slapping the cow's hind quarters.

Haze, which hides, can also reveal. Dips and ravines are discerned in what had appeared a single hill: new depth is given to the vista. And in a long line of crags, such as the great southern rampart of Loch Einich, each buttress is picked out like Vandyke lace. Veils of thin mist drifting along the same great loch-face look iridescent as they float between the sun and the red rock.

For the rock of this granite boss is red, its felspar is the pink variety. Crags, boulders and scree alike are weathered to a cold grey, but find the rock where it is newly slashed, or under water, and there is the glow of the red. After a winter of very severe frost, the river sides of the Lairig have a fresh redness. Here and there one can see a bright gash where a lump of rock the size of a house has fallen; and a very little searching beneath reveals the fallen mass, with one side fresh, or broken into bright red fragments; while nearby is a dark boulder that has lain there for long enough, but from which a red chip has now been struck by the impact of the falling rock.

Or under water: the Beinnie Coire of Braeriach is the least imposing of all the corries – a mere huddle of grey scree. But through it runs a burn that has the effect of sunshine, so red are the stones it hurries over. Farther along the same mountain face, through the deep clear water of Loch Coire an Lochain, even when a thin mist quite covers it, the stones at the bottom are still intense and bright, as though the water itself held radiance. All round the margin of this exquisite loch is a rim of red stones, where the lapping of the water has prevented the growth of lichen.

Thin mist, through which the sun is suffused, gives the mountain a tenuous and ghost-like beauty; but when the mist thickens, one walks in a blind world. And that is bad: though there is a thrill in its eeriness, and a sound satisfaction in not getting lost. For not getting lost is a matter of the mind – of keeping one's head, of having map and compass to hand and knowing how to use them, of staying steady, even when one of the party panics and wants to go in the wrong direction. Walking in mist tests not only individual self-discipline, but the best sort of interplay between persons.

When the mist turns to rain, there may be beauty there too. Like shifting mists, driving rain has a beauty of shape and movement. But there is a kind of rain without beauty, when air and ground are sodden, sullen black rain that invades body and soul alike. It gets down the neck and up the arms and into the boots. One is wet to the skin, and everything one carries has twice its weight. Then the desolation of these empty stretches of land strikes at one's heart. The mountain becomes a monstrous place.

I think the plateau is never quite so desolate as in some days of early spring, when the snow is rather dirty, perished in places like a worn dress; and where it has disappeared, bleached grass, bleached and rotted berries and grey fringe-moss and lichen appear, the moss lifeless, as though its elasticity had gone. The foot sinks in and the impression remains. One can see in it the slot of deer that have passed earlier. This seems to me chiller than unbroken snow.

But even in this scene of grey desolation, if the sun comes out and the wind rises, the eye may suddenly perceive a miracle of beauty. For on the ground the down of a ptarmigan's breast feather has caught the sun. Light blows through it, so transparent the fugitive spindrift feather has become. It blows away and vanishes.

Or in a drab season, and feeling as drab as the weather, I stand on a bridge above a swollen stream. And suddenly the world is made new. Submerged but erect in the margin of the stream I see a tree hung with light – a minimal tree, but exquisite, its branches delicate with globes of light that sparkle under the water. I clamber down and thrust a sacrilegious hand into the stream: I am holding a sodden and shapeless thing. I slip it again under the water and instantly again it is a tree of light. I take it out and examine it: it is a spring of square-stalked St John's Wort, a plant whose leaves are covered with minute pores that can exude a film of oil, protecting it against the water that has engulfed it, in like manner as the dipper plunging into the stream has a film of light between him and the water. I think of the Silver Bough of Celtic mythology and marvel that an enchantment can be made from so small a matter.

Storm in the air wakes the hidden fires – lightning, the electric flickers we call *fire flauchts*, and the Aurora Borealis. Under these alien lights the mountains are remote. They withdraw in the darkness. For even in a night that has neither moon nor stars the mountains can still be seen. The sky cannot be wholly dark. In the most overcast night it is much lighter than the earth; and even the highest hills seem low against the immense night sky. A flash of lightning will draw them close for a brief moment out of this remoteness.

In the darkness one may touch fires from the earth itself. Sparks fly round one's feet as the nails strike rock, and sometimes, if one disturbs black ooze in passing, there leap in it minute pricks of phosphorescent light.

Walking in the dark, oddly enough, can reveal new knowledge about a familiar place. In a moonless week, with overcast skies and wartime blackout, I walked night after night over the moory path from Whitewell to Upper Tullochgrue to hear the news broadcast. I carried a torch but used it only once, when I completely failed to find the gate to the Tullochgrue field. Two pine trees that stood out against the sky were my signposts, and no matter how dark the night the sky was always appreciably lighter than the trees. The heather through which the path runs was very black, the path perceptibly paler, clumps and ridges of heather between the ruts showing dark against the stone and beaten earth. But it amazed me to find how unfamiliar I was with that path. I had followed it times without number, yet now, when my eyes were in my feet, I did not know its bumps and holes, nor where the trickles of water crossed it, nor where it rose and fell. It astonished me that my memory was so much in the eye and so little in the feet, for I am not awkward in the dark and walk easily and happily in it. Yet here I am stumbling because the rock has made a hump in the ground. To be a blind man, I see, needs application.

As I reach the highest part of my dark moor, the world seems to fall away all round, as though I have come to its edge, and were about to walk over. And far off, on a low horizon, the high mountains, the great Cairgorm group, look small as a drystone dyke between two fields.

Apparent size is not only a matter of humidity. It may be

relative to something else in the field of vision. Thus I have seen a newly-risen moon (a harvest moon and still horned), low in the sky, upright, enormous, dwarfing the hills.

SEVEN

Life: The Plants

I have written of inanimate things, rock and water, frost and sun; and it might seem as though this were not a living world. But I have wanted to come to the living things through the forces that create them, for the mountain is one and indivisible, and rock, soil, water and air are no more integral to it than what grows from the soil and breathes the air. All are aspects of one entity, the living mountain. The disintegrating rock, the nurturing rain, the quickening sun, the seed, the root, the bird – all are one. Eagle and alpine veronica are part of the mountain's wholeness. Saxifrage – the 'rock-breaker' – in some of its loveliest forms, *Stelloris*, that stars with its single blossoms the high rocky corrie burns, and *Azoides*, that clusters like soft sunshine in their lower reaches, cannot live apart from the mountain. As well expect the eyelid to function if cut from the eye.

Yet in the terrible blasting winds on the plateau one marvels that life can exist at all. It is not high, as height goes. Plants live far above 4000 feet. But here there is no shelter – or only such shelter as is afforded where the threads of water run in their wide sloping channels towards the edge of the cliffs. Whatever grows, grows in exposure to the whole vast reach of the air. From Iceland, from Norway, from America, from the Pyrenees, the winds tear over it. And on its own undulating surface no rocks, or deep ravines, provide a quiet place for growth. Yet the botanist with whom I sometimes walk tells me that well over twenty species of plant grow there – many more, if each variety of moss, lichen and algae is counted. He has made me a list of them, and I can count them. Life, it seems, won't be warned off.

The tenacity of life can be seen not only on the tops but on lower shoulders where the heather has been burnt. Long before the heather itself (whose power to survive fire as well as frost, wind, and all natural inclemencies is well known) shows the least sign of life from the roots beneath its charred sticks, or has sprouted anew from seed hidden in the ground, birdsfoot trefoil, tormentil, blaeberry, the tiny genista, alpine lady's mantle, are thrusting up vigorous shoots. These mountain flowers look inexpressibly delicate; their stems are slender, their blossoms fragile; but burrow a little in the soil, and roots of a timeless endurance are found. Squat or stringy, like lumps of dead wood or bits of sinew, they conserve beneath the soil the vital energy of the plant. Even when all the upper growth is stripped – burned or frosted or withered away – these knots of life are everywhere. There is no time nor season when the mountain is not alive with them. Or if the root has perished, living seeds are in the soil, ready to begin the cycle of life afresh. Nowhere more than here is life proved invincible. Everything is against it, but it pays no heed.

The plants of the plateau are low in stature, sitting tight to the ground with no loose ends for the wind to catch. They creep, either along the surface, or under it; or they anchor

themselves by a heavy root massive out of all proportion to
their external growth. I have said that they have no shelter,
but for the individual flower there is the shelter of its group.
Thus the moss campion, *Silene*, the most startling of all the
plateau flowers, that in June and early July amazes the eye by
its cushions of brilliant pink scattered in the barest and most
stony places, has a habit of growth as close-set as a Victorian
posy. Its root too is strong and deep, anchoring it against the
hurricane, and keeping its vital essence safe against frost and
fiery drought, the extremes and unpredictable shifts of weather
on the exposed plateau. In these ways this most characteristic
of the plateau flowers is seen to be quite simply a part of the
mountain. Its way of life lies in the mountain's way of life as
water lies in a channel.

Even its flamboyant flowers are integral to the mountain's
way of life. I do not know how old the individual clumps may
be, but judging from the size to which these close-knit cushions grow, some must have endured the commotion of many
winters. Most of the mountain flowers are long livers. The
plant that races through its cycle in a single season could
never be sure, up here, of fruition – there might be no success-
ors. Death would dog, not only the individual, but the species.
Yet even the long livers must renew themselves at times, and
it is on only some of the summer days that insects can fly to
the mountain top. So the *Silene* throws this ardent colour into
its petals to entice the flies.

Lower on the mountain, on all the slopes and shoulders
and ridges and on the moors below, the characteristic growth
is heather. And this too is integral to the mountain. For
heather grows in its most profuse luxuriance on granite, so

that the very substance of the mountain is in its life. Of the three varieties that grow on these hills – two Ericas and the ling – the July-blooming bell heather is the least beautiful, though its clumps of hot red are like sun-bursts when the rest of the hills are still brown. The pale cross-leaved heath, that grows in small patches, often only single heads, in moist places, is an exquisite, almost waxen-still, with a honey perfume. But it is the August-blooming ling that covers the hills with amethyst. Now they look gracious and benign. For many many miles there is nothing but this soft radiance. Walk over it in a hot sun, preferably not on a path ('I like the unpath best,' one of my small friends said when her father had called her to heel), and the scent rises in a heady cloud. Just as one walks on a hot day surrounded by one's own aura of flies, so one walks surrounded by one's own aura of heather scent. For as the feet brush the bloom, the pollen rises in a perfumed cloud. It settles on one's boots, or if one is walking barefoot, on feet and legs, yellowy-fawn in colour, silky to the touch, yet leaving a perceptible grit between the fingers. Miles of this, however, stupefies the body. Like too much incense in church, it blunts the sharp edge of adoration, which, at its finest, demands clarity of the intellect as well as the surge of emotion.

To one who loves the hills at every season, the blossoming is not the best of the heather. The best of it is simply its being there – is the feel of it under the feet. To feel heather under the feet after long abstinence is one of the dearest joys I know.

Scent – fragrance, perfume – is very much pertinent to the theme of life, for it is largely a by-product of the process of living. It may also be a by-product of fire, but then fire feeds on what lives or what has lived. Or of chemical action, but if there are obscure chemical processes at work in the dead stuff of the mountain, they give little indication to my nose. The smells I smell are of life, plant and animal. Even the good smell of earth, one of the best smells in the world, is a smell of life, because it is the activity of bacteria in it that sets up this smell.

Plants then, as they go through the business of living, emit odours. Some, like the honey scents of flowers, are an added allurement to the insects; and if, as with heather, the scent is poured out most recklessly in the heat of the sun, that is because it is then that the insects are out in strength. But in other cases – as the fir trees – the fragrance is the sap, is the very life itself. When the aromatic savour of the pine goes searching into the deepest recesses of my lungs, I know it is life that is entering. I draw life in through the delicate hairs of my nostrils. Pines, like heather, yield their fragrance to the sun's heat. Or when the foresters come, and they are cut, then their scent is strong. Of all the kinds that grow on the low reaches of these mountains, spruce throws the strongest perfume on the air when the saw goes through it. In hot sun it is almost like a ferment – like strawberry jam on the boil, but with a tang that tautens the membranes of nose and throat.

Of plants that carry their fragrance in their leaves, bog myrtle is the mountain exampler. This grey-green shrub fills the boggy hollows, neighboured by cotton grass and sundew, bog asphodel and the spotted orchis, and the minute scarlet cups of the lichens. Its fragrance is cool and clean, and like the wild thyme it gives it most strongly when crushed.

The other shrub, juniper, is secretive with its scent. It has an odd habit of dying in patches, and when a dead branch is snapped, a spicy odour comes from it. I have carried a piece of juniper wood for months, breaking it afresh now and then to renew the spice. This dead wood has a grey silk skin, impervious to rain. In the wettest season, when every fir branch in the woods is sodden, the juniper is crackling dry and burns with a clear heat. There's nothing better under the girdle when scones are baking unless perhaps small larch twigs, fed into a fire already banked. Once, striking thick loose snow from low juniper bushes before walking through them, I surprised myself by striking from them also a delectable fragrance, that floated on the wintry air.

Birch, the other tree that grows on the lower mountain slopes, needs rain to release its odour. It is a scent with body to it, fruity like old brandy, and on a wet warm day, one can be as good as drunk with it. Acting through the sensory nerves, it confuses the higher centres; one is excited, with no cause that the wit can define.

Birch trees are least beautiful when fully clothed. Exquisite when the opening leaves just fleck them with points of green flame, or the thinning leaves turn them to a golden lace, they are loveliest of all when naked. In a low sun, the spun silk floss of their twigs seems to be created out of light. Without transfiguration, they are seen to be purple – when the sap is rising, a purple so glowing that I have caught sight of a birchwood on a hillside and for one incredulous moment thought the heather was in bloom.

Among drifts of these purple glowing birches, an occasional rowan looks dead; its naked boughts are a smooth white-grey, almost ghastly as the winter light runs over them. The rowan's moment is in October, when even the warmth of its clustering berries is surpassed by the blood-red brilliance of its leaves. This is the 'blessed quicken wood', that has power against the spirits of evil. It grows here and there among birches and firs, as a rule singly, and sometimes higher than either, a solitary bush by the rivulet in a ravine.

October is the coloured month here, far more brilliant than June, blazing more sharply than August. From the gold of the birches and bracken on the low slopes, the colour spurts upwards through all the creeping and inconspicuous growths that live among the heather roots – mosses that are lush green, or oak-brown, or scarlet, and the berried plants, blaeberry, cranberry, crowberry and the rest. Blaeberry leaves are a flaming crimson, and they are loveliest of all in the Rothie-murchus Forest, where the fir trees were felled in the 1914 War, and round and out of each stump blaeberry grows in upright sprigs: so that in October a multitude of pointed flames seem to burn upwards all over the moor.

This forest blazed with real fire in the early summer of 1920. One of the gamekeepers told me that forty of them were on the watch for ten days and nights, to keep the fire from spreading. And by night, he said, the tree trunks glowed like pillars of fire.

Not much is left now of this great pine forest. Yet in the glens that run up into the mountain, there are still a few of the very old firs that may have been the original Caledonian forest. Old trees still stand in Glen Einich, as they do at Ballochbuie on the other side of the mountain; and by the shores of Loch an Eilein are a scatter of enormous venerable Scots firs, their girth two and a half times the span of my (quite long) arms, the flakes of their bark a foot and a half in length and thick as books, their roots, exposed where the soil has been washed away above the path, twisted and intertwined like a cage of snakes. Here and there also, notably by the sluice gates at the exit of Loch Einich, can be seen, half-sunk in the bog, numbers of the roots of trees long perished.

This sluice dates, like those on other of the lochs, to the late eighteenth century, when the ancient wood rang with the activity of the fellers. The trunks ready, the sluices were opened, and the trees guided down on the rush of water to the Spey. There is a vivid description of it, as a child remembered it, in Elizabeth Grant of Rothiemurchus's *Memoirs of a Highland Lady*. When the timber was first realised to be a source of wealth, and felled, small sawmills were erected on the various burns – tiny clearings, with the saw, a but and a ben and a patch of corn; but soon it was found more profitable to float all the timber downstream to the Spey, where it was made into rough rafts and so carried to Fochabers and Garmouth. The very sites of these ancient sawmills are forgotten. Today come the motor lorries, the sawmill and all its machinery making a compact township for the time that it is required; and outsiders, not the men of the place, fell and lop and cut. Only the old ways still linger here and there as where a native horse, tended by a man deep-rooted in the place, drags the chained trunks down from inaccessible corners, and is led back for the night to one of the ancient farms on the edge of the moor.

The first great cutting of the forest took place during the Napoleonic wars, when home-grown timber was urgently required. A century later we have seen the same thing happen.

In 1914 and again, and more drastically, in 1940, the later wood has gone the way of the former. It will grow again, but for a while the land will be scarred and the living things – the crested tits, the shy roe deer – will flee. I tremble especially for the crested tit, whose rarity is a proud distinction of these woods.

I have heard people say that they have watched in vain for these exquisite tits, but, if you know their haunts (I shall not give them away), they can be conjured easily from a tree by simply standing still against its trunk. You have heard the stir and small sound of tits, but at your approach they are gone, there is not a bird to see. But stand quite still, and in a minute or two they forget you, and flit from branch to branch close to your head. I have seen a crested tit turn itself around not a foot from my eye. In the nesting season, however, they will scold like fishwives. I have been scolded at by a pair of them with such vehemence that in pure shame for them I have left their tree.

How fierce was the rush of water when the ancient sluices on the lochs were opened an eighty-year-old woman made plain to me when she told me how it was once used to outwit the gauger. For a drop of the mountain dew was made on the far side of the Beinnie, in a thick place beneath Carn Elrig where I once lost my path; and when the man who made it had the word passed to him that the gauger was on the way, he had no time to hide the stuff. Indeed, then, when the word came to him, he was nearer the sluice than the still, and to the sluice he went – I can see him *spangin'* on, heel to the ground, with the loping stride of the Highlander bent on business. So when the exciseman came, turbulent water raced between him and the drop whisky. And no crossing it that day at the least. Nor perhaps the next.

Gaunt remnants of pine trees high on the mountain sides show that the earlier forest went further up than the present forest does. Yet here and there a single seed, wind borne or dropped by a bird, has grown far above the main body of the trees. Some of these out-liers show the amazing adaptability of this tree. They can change their form at need, like any wizard. I know one, rooted a few paces from a 2900 feet summit, a sturdy plant but splayed to the mountains and almost roseate in structure, three feet across and not more than five inches in height. There it clings, plastered against the arid ground. I shall watch with much interest to see how much larger it will grow, and in what direction.

Dead fir roots, left in the soil long after the tree is gone, make the best kindling in the world. I know old women who look with the utmost contempt on paper as a fire-lighter and scorn to use more than one match to set a fire going. I know two such old women, both well over eighty, both living alone, one on the Spey side of the mountains and one on the Dee, who howk their fir roots from the moor, drag them home and splinter them. Then you may watch them, if you visit their frugal homes when the fire is out, build the *rossity reets* (we call them that on the Aberdeenshire side) into a pyramid with their brown hard wrinkled fingers, fill the kettle with a cup from the pail of well water, hang it on the *swye* and swing it over the blazing sticks. And before you have well settled to your *newse* the tea is made, and if the brown earthenware teapot has a broken spout ('my teapot has lost a tooth'), and tea splutters from it on to the open hearth and raises spurts of ash and steam, you can call it a *soss* or a libation to the gods as you feel inclined, but it will not make the tea less good nor the talk less racy.

Of the inconspicuous things that creep in heather, I have a special affection for stagmoss – not the hard braided kind but the fuzzy kind we called 'toadstails'. I was taught the art of picking these by my father when I was a small child. We lay on the heather and my fingers learned to feel their way along each separate trail and side branch, carefully detaching each tiny root, until we had thick bunchy pieces many yards long. It was a good art to teach a child. Though I did not know it then, I was learning my way in, through my own fingers, to the secret of growth.

That secret the mountain never quite gives away. Man is slowly learning to read it. He watches, he ponders, patiently he adds fact to fact. He finds a hint of it in the 'formidable' roots of the moss campion and in the fine roots that the tiny eyebright sends into the substance of the grass to ease its own search for food. It is in the glaucous and fleshy leaves of the sedums and the saxifrages, through which they store the bounty of the earth against the times when the earth is not bountiful. It is in the miniature size of the smallest willow, whose woolly fluff blows about the plateau as the silky hairs of the cotton grass blow about the bogs. And in the miniature azalea that grows splayed against the mountain for protection, and lures the rare insects by its rosy hue, and flourishes, like the heather, on granite; whereas granite cannot meet the needs of many of the rare mountain flowers, that crave the streaks of lime-stone, or the rich humus of the micaschist – like that rarest of all, found in only one spot in the Cairngorms, the alpine milk-vetch, its delicate pale bloom edged with lavender, haunted by its red-and-black familiar the Burnet moth: why so haunted no one knows, but no milk-vetch, no Burnet moth. On a wet windy sunless day, when moths would hardly be expected to be visible at all, we have found numbers of these tart little creatures on the milk-vetch clumps.

The more one learns of this intricate interplay of soil, altitude, weather, and the living tissues of plant and insect (an intricacy that has its astonishing moments, as when sundew and butterwort eat the insects), the more the mystery deepens. Knowledge does not dispel mystery. Scientists tell me that the alpine flora of the Scottish mountains is Arctic in origin – that these small scattered plants have outlived the Glacial period and are the only vegetable life in our country that is older than the Ice Age. But that doesn't explain them. It only adds time to the equation and gives it a new dimension. I find I have a naive faith in my scientist friends – they are such jolly people, they wouldn't fib to me unnecessarily, and their stories make the world so interesting. But my imagination boggles at this. I can imagine the antiquity of rock, but the antiquity of a living flower – that is harder. It means that these toughs of the mountain top, with their angelic inflorescence and the devil in their roots, have had the cunning and the effrontery to cheat, not only a winter, but an Ice Age. The scientists have the humility to acknowledge that they don't know how it has been done.

EIGHT

Life: Birds, Animals, Insects

The first time I found summer on the plateau – for although my earliest expeditions were all made in June or July, I experienced cloud, mist, howling wind, hailstones, rain and even a blizzard – the first time the sun blazed and the air was balmy, we were standing on the edge of an outward facing precipice, when I was startled by a whizzing sound behind me. Something dark swished past the side of my head at a speed that made me giddy. Hardly had I got back my balance when it came again, whistling through the windless air, which eddied round me with the motion. This time my eyes were ready, and I realised that a swift was sweeping in mighty curves over the edge of the plateau, plunging down the face of the rock and rising again like a jet of water. No one had told me I should find swifts on the mountain. Eagles and ptarmigan, yes: but that first sight of the mad, joyous abandon of the swift over and over the very edge of the precipice shocked me with a thrill of elation. All that volley of speed, those convolutions of delight, to catch a few flies! The discrepancy between purpose and performance made me laugh aloud – a laugh that gave the same feeling of release as though I had been dancing for a long time.

It seems odd that merely to watch the motion of flight should give the body not only vicarious exhilaration but release. So urgent is the rhythm that it invades the blood. This power of flight to take us in to itself through the eyes as though we had actually shared in the motion, I have never felt so strongly as when watching swifts on the mountain top. Their headlong rush, each curve of which is at the same time a miracle of grace, the swishing sound of their cleavage of the air and the occasional high pitched cry that is hardly like the note of an earthly bird, seem to make visible and audible some essence of the free, wild spirit of the mountain.

The flight of the eagle, if less immediately exciting than that of the swifts, is more profoundly satisfying. The great spiral of his ascent, rising coil over coil in slow symmetry, has in its movement all the amplitude of space. And when he has soared to the top of his bent, there comes the level flight as far as the eye can follow, straight, clean and effortless as breathing. The wings hardly move, now and then perhaps a lazy flap as though a cyclist, free-wheeling on a gentle slope, turned the crank a time or two. The bird seems to float, but to float with a direct and undeviating force. It is only when one remarks that he is floating up-wind that the magnitude of that force becomes apparent. I stood once about the 2500 feet level, in January when the world was quite white, and watched an eagle well below me following up the river valley in search of food. He flew right into the wind. The wings were slightly tilted, but so far as I could judge from above he held them steady. And he came on with a purposeful urgency behind which must have been the very terror of strength.

It was this strong undeviating flight on steady wings that

made a member of the Observer Corps (my friend James McGregor reports – the Observation Post was in his highest field and his croft, I believe, is the highest in Scotland) cry out in excitement, 'Here's a plane I can't identify! What's this one, do you think?' McGregor looked and said, without a glimmer, 'That's the one they call the Golden Eagle.' 'Didn't know there was such a one,' said the other; and he could hardly be convinced that he was looking at a bird and not a plane. And just this morning, in my own garden on Lower Deeside, fifty miles from the eagle country, I caught sight of three planes very high against white clouds, wheeling in circles round one another, and my first amazed reaction was 'Eagles!'

Mr Seton Gordon claims that the Golden Eagle rises from her eyrie clumsily, especially when the air is calm. I have never had, I was going to say the luck, but I should say rather the assiduity and patience to see an eagle rising from the eyrie, but I have watched one fly out from the vicinity of an eyrie, alight in heather some distance away, rise again and again alight, and there was nothing noteworthy in its movement. It is the power in the flight that enthrals the eye. And when one has realised, as probably one does not do at first, that it is a power which binds the strength of the wind to its own purpose, so that the more powerful the wind the more powerful is the flight of the bird, then one sees how intimately the eagle, like the moss campion, is integral to the mountain. Only here, where the wind tears across these desolate marches, can it prove the utmost of its own strength.

To see the Golden Eagle at close quarters requires knowledge and patience – though sometimes it may be a gift, as when once, just as I reached a summit cairn, an eagle rose from the far side of it and swept up in majestic circles above my head: I have never been nearer to the king of birds. And once, on the edge of the Braeriach side of the Lairig crags, I saw an eagle soar out below me, glinting golden in the sun. And I have seen one near on a hillside, intent on something at his feet. But getting close to him is a slow art. One spring afternoon, while I was idling among the last trees on the Speyside end of the Lairig path, watching the movement of tits, a voice by my side asked: 'Is this the way to Ben MacDhui?' and looking down I saw what at first glance I took to be a street gamin of eleven. I said, 'Are you going up alone?' and he said, 'I'm with him.' So turning I saw behind me a second youth, lanky, pasty and pimply, hung round with gadgets. They were both, perhaps, even the undergrown one, nineteen years of age, and they were railway workers who had come all the way from Manchester to spend their one week's leave in photographing the Golden Eagle. And please, where would they find one? I told them of some of my encounters. 'And could you have photographed that one?' they asked. They knew, I found, the books. Those two weedy boys had read everything they could find on their subject, and though they had never been in Scotland before, they had walked in the Lakes. 'The distances,' I said, 'are different. Don't try Ben MacDhui till tomorrow, and take the whole day to it.' And I remembered an old shepherd in Galloway, whom I had asked which spur of the hill I should take to go up Merrick. When he had told me, he looked at me, and said, 'You've not been up before? Do you know what you're undertaking?' 'I've not been up before, but I've been all over the Cairngorms.' 'The Cairngorms, have you?' His gesture dismissed me – it was like a

63

drawbridge thrown forward. So I said to the boys, 'Don't go up Ben MacDhui today – it'll be dark in another four or five hours. Go on by the path you're on and see the Pools of Dee and perhaps look around the corner into the great Garbh Coire.' 'Will there be ledges there?' they asked; and repeated that what they had come for was to photograph the Golden Eagle. I never saw them again – I hope I dissuaded them from going up Ben MacDhui that day – I didn't even attempt to dissuade them from photographing the Golden Eagle. The eagle itself probably did that quite effectively. But I liked those boys. I hope they saw an eagle. Their informed enthusiasm – even if only half informed – was the right way in.

Imagination is haunted by the swiftness of the creatures that live on the mountain – eagle and peregrine falcon, red deer and mountain hare. The reason for their swiftness is severely practical: food is so scarce up there that only those who can move swiftly over vast stretches of ground may hope to survive. The speed, the whorls and torrents of movement, are in plain fact the mountain's own necessity. But their grace is not necessity. Or if it is – if the swoop, the parabola, the arrow-flight of hooves and wings achieve their beauty by strict adherence to the needs of function – so much the more is the mountain's integrity vindicated. Beauty is not adventitious but essential.

Strong flight is a characteristic also of another bird that haunts not the precipice but the plateau itself – the small unassuming dotterel. You are wandering one summer day on a plateau slope when your ear catches its plover-like cry. You pause and watch – no bird is there. Then you move softly towards the sound, and in a moment one bird, then another, rises in short low flight, comes to earth again and runs, crouched to the ground like a small grey mouse. Shape, movement, colour, are all so mouse-like that the illusion almost might deceive you, were it not for the vivid black and white of the head, the glowing breast, and the white tail feathers. You wait, and soon the birds forget you. On one slope, off the recognised route to any particular destination, a nesting place or perhaps a gathering place for flight, of these small birds, I have seen them by the score, running a little way, and pausing, and running on again, almost domestic in their simple movements. Yet in autumn this humble bird flies straight to Africa.

The other bird that nests on the high plateau, the ptarmigan, is a home-keeper. No flights to Africa for him. Through the most ferocious winter, he stays where he was born, perhaps a little lower on the slopes, and dressed for winter by changing to the colour of the snow.

The creatures that dress like the snow to be inconspicuous against it – the ptarmigan, the snow bunting, the mountain hare – are sometimes cheated. They are white before the mountain is. When blue milkwort is still in blossom on the last day of the year, it is not surprising to see a white stoat blaze against a dull grey dyke. Few things are more ludicrous in Nature than a white hare 'concealing' itself, erect and patient beside a boulder, while all round it stretches a grey-brown world against which it stands vividly out. A white hare running over snow can be comical too, if it is running between you and the sun – a shadowed shape, with an odd ludicrous leggy shadow-skeleton, comical because the shadows alter the creature's shape. But if the sun is behind you and strikes full on the running hare, only the ears show, and a dark thin outline to the back. If the snow lies in fields, the running hare may not be noticed at all, till it flakes off at the edge of the snow patch, gleaming white. Breaking suddenly into a hollow, I have counted twenty white hares at a time streaking up a brown hillside like rising smoke.

Deer on the other hand are conspicuous in snow. In a completely white world, one can see from a high shoulder a herd feeding a thousand feet beneath, vivid black specks on the whiteness. But then they do not need to hide themselves from peregrine and eagle. Actually in winter and early spring, their coats are greyish, the colour of dead snow, bleached heather and juniper and rocks.

Stay-at-home though he be, the ptarmigan has power in his wings. In startled flight, his wing-beats are so rapid that the white wings lose all appearance of solidity, they are like an aura of light around the body.

Like all the game birds, ptarmigan play the broken wing trick when an intruder approaches their young family, to lure the enemy away. I have had the trick played on me so many times that now I hardly notice the parent birds, but always and eagerly I watch the behaviour of the young. Once near the summit of Braeriach, I halted dead at the rise of one, then the other parent, seeking with my eyes for the youngsters. There was one, three feet away, another nearer, and another. My eyes came closer and closer to myself – one ptarmigan chick was not two inches from my boot. Seven of them crouched within a radius of a foot or two, and they might have been birds carved from wood for all the life they showed. I stood for a long time and as long as I remained motionless, so did they. But at last I yielded to the mounting temptation (which I try always to resist) to touch and fondle one of these morsels. So I stooped to the one nearest my boot. And instantly the whole seven, cackling, were off. A noisy undignified scramble, contrasting strangely with their carved immobility.

Very near the summits, on the most stony braes nest the snow buntings. Both in song and in person these small creatures have a delicate perfection that is enhanced by the savagery of their home. Sit quietly for a while in some of the loneliest and most desolate crannies of the mountain, where the imagination is overpowered by grim bastions of the rock, and a single snow bunting will sing with incredible sweetness beside you. To have sat on one of the high stony fields around seven of a clear summer morning, when the sun has just drawn up the morning mists from the corries, and seen the stones come alive with small forms like flakes of the stone blown eddying upon the air, is to have tasted a pleasure of the epicure. Watching carefully, one sees that two of the dozen or so birds are males, the rest are the members of their two young families. The females are already about the business of bringing out a second brood.

Ranging the whole mountain mass are the hoodies, black and grey, the mountain scavengers. Wheatears bob and chuckle on the boulders, or flash their cheeky rumps as they fly to another stone. And in the burns of the highest corries the white-dickied dipper plunges beneath the water. A lonely song by a solitary burn reveals the golden plover. But why should I make a list? It serves no purpose, and they are all in the books. But they are not in the books for me – they are in living encounters, moments of their life that have crossed moments of mine. They are in the cry of the curlew sounding over the distances, and in the thin silver singing among the last trees that tell me the tits are there. They are in an April morning when I follow a burn to its sources, further and further into a fold of the hills, and a pair of long-tailed tits flash and are gone and come again. Or in a December afternoon of bitter frost when a dozen of these tiny tufts, disproportionate and exquisite, tumble from a tree beside a frozen stream. Or a July day when one small tree holds thirteen crested tits. Or in a March day (the only time I have found anything attractive in the grouse) when against the snowy hillside a pair of these birds pursued each other in lovely patterns of flight. Or in the mating ecstasy of the kestrel, or the fighting blackcock suddenly discovered one morning in a clear place among juniper. Or in the two woodcock that follow each other night after night low over the trees just beyond where I lie still awake outside the tent.

And so many that I have omitted. Just as I have omitted so many exquisite flowers – dryas, timeless as white jade, bog asphodel like candle flame, the purple-black hearts of cornel. I have missed the wagtails, yellow and pied, and the reed bunting precise as a dignitary in his bands, the seagulls and oyster catchers come up from the sea, the crossbills and the finches, and the wrens. But I cannot miss the wrens. So tiny, so vital, with such volume of voice. It may not be fact, but in my experience the wrens are more numerous on the Dee side of the range than on the Spey side. In the high tributary valleys, Glen Quoich, Glen Slugain, among the last of the trees, they are common as eyebright. There's a skeleton of a fallen tree in Glen Quoich, a vast leggy thing, all the legs to the ground and the trunk a ridge of spine above them, a magnificent example of prevailing wind – twinkling through its bony ribs I have watched a family of nine young wrens. And once in Glen Slugain a pair of golden bumble bees (as it seemed) sped past me in a whorl of joyful speed. But it couldn't be – they were too large. I stalked them. They were young wrens.

It was near the leggy tree that I saw rise some way off down the stream, a bird so huge that I could only stare. It wheeled and vanished. Two enormous wings, with a span that I couldn't believe. Yet I had seen it. And there it was coming back, upstream now, the same vast span of wing: no body that I could see; two great wings joined by nothing, as though some bird had at last discovered how to be all flight and no body. And then I saw. The two great wings were a duck and a drake, following one another in perfect formation, wheeling and dipping and rising again with an unchanging interval of space between them, each following every modulation of the other; two halves of one organism.

Wild geese are only passers here. One blustering October day I watched an arrow-head of them, twenty-seven birds in perfect symmetry, flying south down the valley in which I stood. I was near the head of a deep glen, the watershed rose steep above me. Up there the wind must be ferocious. The geese were there now. They broke formation. Birds flew from one arm of the wedge to the other, the leader hesitated, another bird attempted to lead, their lovely symmetry became confused. It seemed as though the wind were beating them back, for the whole line, blunt-headed now, edged round, one bird leading and then another, till they gradually rounded the top of the glen and were flying back the way they came. As I watched, they flew into a cinder-grey cloud, in an undulating line like the movement of a fish under water. The dark line melted into the darkness of the cloud, and I could not tell where or when they resumed formation and direction.

It is tantalising to see something unusual, but not its ending. One January afternoon, in a frozen silent world, I saw two stags with antlers interlaced dragging each other backwards and forwards across the ringing frozen floor of a hollow. Their dark forms stood out against the snow. I watched till dusk came on and I could barely see but could still hear the noise of the scuffle. It is the only time I have seen this phenomenon of interlocked antlers, and as I have always been told that stags so caught cannot extricate themselves and fight on till one or both die, I wanted badly to see what happened. I went back next day but found no stags, dead or alive. The crofter-ghillie in whose house I was staying said that they probably saved themselves by the breaking of an antler.

The roaring of the stags set me another problem to which I have not found a definitive answer. On one of those potent days of mid-October, golden as whisky, I was wandering on the slopes of Ben Avon above Loch Builg. Suddenly I was startled by a musical call that resounded across the hill, and was answered by a like call from another direction. Yodelling, I thought. There was such gaiety in the sound that I looked eagerly about, thinking: these are students, they are hailing one another from sheer exuberance of spirit. But I saw no one. The yodelling went on. The yodelling went on all day, clear, bell-like and musical; and it was not long till I realised that there was no other human being on the mountain and that the stags were the yodellers. The clear bell notes were new to me. I had heard stags roar often enough, in deep raucous tones. Bellowing. The dictionary would have me believe that belling is merely a variant of bellowing. For me belling will always mean the music of that golden day. All the time I listened, there was not a single harsh note.

But why? That is what I don't understand. Why sometimes raucous and sometimes like a bell? Hillmen whom I have asked give different suggestions. That the bell notes are from young stags and the raucous from old. But against that, one gamekeeper sets the tale of a gruff-voiced bellower that the shooting-party to a man declared would be an old beast and that turned out when they got him to be comparatively young. That the note changes to express different needs. But that theory does not seem to be borne out by the way in which two stags kept up an antiphon one day in my hearing, the raucous answering the bell across a ravine with absolute consistency. That stags are like human beings and some have tenor voices, some bass. Then were they all tenor stags on that morning when the hill broke into a cantata? All young? or all tenor? or all in love with the morning?

Normally deer are silent creatures, but when alarmed they bark like an angry dog. I have heard the warning bark far off on a distant slope and only then been aware of the presence of a herd. Then they are off, flowing up the hill and over the horizon. Their patterns against the sky are endless – a quiet frieze of doe and fawn and doe and fawn. Or a tossing forest of massed antlers. Or with long necks to the ground, feeding, like hens pecking. Those mobile necks are a thought uncanny at times. I have seen five necks rise like swaying snakes, a small snake-like head on each, the bodies hidden. Five hinds.

And I have seen a hind turn her head to look at me, twisting her neck round until the face seemed to hang suspended in air alongside the rump and some atavisitic fear awoke in me. Bird, animal and reptile – there is something of them all in the deer. Its flight is fluid as a bird's. Especially the roes, the very young ones, dappled, with limbs like the stalks of flowers, move over the heather with an incredible lightness. They seem to float; yet their motion is in a way more wonderful even than flight, for each of these gleaming hooves does touch the ground. The lovely pattern of the limbs is fixed to the earth and cannot be detached from it.

Indeed there are times when the earth seems to re-absorb this creature of air and light. Roes melt into the wood – I have stared a long time into birches where I knew a doe was standing and saw her only when at last she flicked an ear. In December on open heather I have found myself close upon a feeding red doe so like her background that I had thought the white scut another patch of snow. She becomes aware of me, her ears lift, her head goes sharply up, the neck elongated. I stand very still, the head drops, she becomes again part of the the earth. Further up on the slopes one can watch a fawn learning his hillcraft from his mother, pausing in exactly her attitude, turning a wary head as she turns hers.

But find a fawn alone in a hidden hollow, he will not endure with his mother's patience. It is not easy to make a doe move before you do, but when the fawn, after his first startled jump to the far side of the hollow, stands to gaze at you on the other side, if you keep perfectly still he grows restive, moves his head now side on to you, now front, an ear twitches, a nostril, finally he turns and walks away, like a reluctant but inquisitive child, pausing at every third step to look back.

I have never had the incredible fortune, as a young doctor I know once had, of seeing a hind give birth; but I have found very young fawns, left by their mothers beside a stone on heather. Once I had gone off the track to visit a small tarn. Something impelled me to walk round the back of the tarn, scrambling between the rock and the water, and then to continue downwards over a heathery slope that is not very often crossed. From the corner of my eye I noticed two or three hinds making off; and a moment later I came on a tiny fawn lying crouched into the heather near a stone. It lay in an oddly rigid way, the limbs contorted in unnatural positions. Could it be dead? I bent over it – very gently touched it. It was warm. The contorted limbs were fluid as water in my hands. The little creature gave no sign of life. The neck was stretched, stiff and ungainly, the head almost hidden; the eyes stared, undeviating. Only the flanks pulsated. Nothing moved but the pulsing flanks. There was no voluntary movement whatsoever, no smallest twitch or flicker. I had never before seen a fawn shamming dead, as young birds do.

A young squirrel, caught upon his own occasions, will behave like the young fawn you have surprised walking out alone: both are a little reckless about humanity. I have come upon a small squirrel the size of a well-grown mouse, on the ground under fir trees, scampering from cone to cone, picking up each in turn, scrutinising, sampling, tossing it away, with a sort of wilful petulance in his movements such as I have seen in small children who have too many toys. He becomes aware of me, pauses, eyes me, eyes his cone. Cupidity and caution struggle within him, I am quite still, caution loses, he goes on with his game among the goodies. When he stops to crunch, I move forward. At last I move so near that he is suddenly alarmed. He makes for a huge old pine tree whose bark hangs in scales so thick and solid that his small limbs can hardly compass them. He can't get up; and now, like his red-gold parents, he wallops his thin long ribbon-like tail, not yet grown bushy, in a small futile way, and scrabbles against the mountainous humps of bark. At last he is up, he runs out on a side branch and jeers down at me in triumph.

Other young things – leverets in the form wrapped in silky hair – fox cubs playing in the sun in a distant fold of the hill – the fox himself with his fat red brush – the red-brown squirrel in the woods below, whacking his tail against the tree-trunk and chattering through closed lips (I think) against the intruder – gold-brown lizards and the gold-brown floss of cocoons in the heather – small golden bees and small blue butterflies – green dragon flies and emerald beetles – moths like oiled paper and moths like burnt paper – water-beetles skimming the highest tarns – small mice so rarely seen but leaving a thousand tracks upon the snow – ant-heaps of birch-twigs or pine-needles (*preens*, in the northern word) flickering with activity when the sun shines – midges, mosquitoes, flies by the hundred thousand, adders and a rare strange slowworm – small frogs jumping like tiddly-winks – rich brown hairy caterpillars by the handful and fat green ones with blobs of amethyst, a perfect camouflage on heather – life in so many guises.

It is not just now sheep country. The sheep were cleared to make room for deer; today in one district the deer are giving place to Highland cattle, those placid and abstemious beasts to whom thin fare is a necessity and whose shaggy winter mats protect them from the bitter winds. They look ferocious and are very gentle – in this resembling some of the blackface ewes, hags as ugly as sin that are found in every mountain flock, grim old malignants whose cankered horns above a black physiognomy must, I feel sure, be the origin of the Scots conception of the Devil.

NINE

Life: Man

Up on the plateau nothing has moved for a long time. I have walked all day, and seen no one. I have heard no living sound. Once, in a solitary corrie, the rattle of a falling stone betrayed the passage of a line of stags. But up here, no movement, no voice. Man might be a thousand years away.

Yet, as I look round me, I am touched at many points by his presence. His presence is in the cairns, marking the summits, marking the paths, marking the spot where a man has died, or where a river is born. It is in the paths themselves; even over boulder and rock man's persistent passage can be seen, as at the head of the Lairig Ghru, where the path, over brown-grey weathered and lichened stones, shines as red as new-made rock. It is in the stepping-stones over the burns, and lower in the glens, the bridges. It is in the indicator on Ben MacDhui, planned with patient skill, that gathers the congregation of the hills into the hollow of one's hand; and some few feet below, in the remains of the hut where the men who made the Ordnance Survey of the eighteen-sixties lived for the whole of a season – an old man has told me how down in the valley they used to watch a light glow now from one summit, now another, as measurements were made and checked. Man's presence too is in the map and the compass that I carry, and in the names recorded in the map, ancient Gaelic names that show how old is man's association with scaur and corrie: the Loch of the Thin Man's Son, the Coire of the Cobbler, the Dairymaid's Meadow, the Lurcher's Crag. It is in the hiding-holes of hunted men, Argyll's Stone on Creag Dhubh above Glen Einich, and the Cat's Den, deep narrow chasm among the Kennapol rocks; and in the Thieves' Road that runs south from Nethy through prehistoric glacial overflow gaps – and somewhere on its way the kent tree (felled now) to which the prudent landlord tied a couple of his beasts as clearance money. It is in the sluices at the outflow of the lochs, the remnants of lime kilns by the burns, and the shepherds' huts, roofless now, and the bothies of which nothing remains but a chimney-gable; and in the Shelter Stone above Loch Avon, reputed once to have been the den of a gang some thirty strong, before the foundation stones that hold the immense perched rock shifted and the space beneath was narrowed to its present dimensions: wide enough still to hold a half-dozen sleepers, whose names, like the names of hundreds of others, are recorded in a book wrapped in waterproof and left within the shelter of the cave.

Man's presence too is disturbingly evident, in these latter days, in the wrecked aeroplanes that lie scattered over the mountains. During the Second World War more planes (mostly training planes) crashed here than one cares to remember. Like the unwary of older days who were drowned while fording swollen streams, or dashed from the precipices they attempted to climb, these new travellers underestimated the mountain's power. Its long flat plateau top has a deceptive air of lowness;

and its mists shut down too swiftly, its tops are too often swathed in cloud, pelting rain or driving snow, while beneath the world is in clear sunlight, for liberties to be taken with its cruel rock. I stood one day on the Lurcher's Crag and heard the engine of a plane, and looked naturally upwards; but in a moment I realised that the sound was below me. A plane was edging its way steadily through the great gash that separates the two halves of the plateau, the Lairig Ghru. From where I stood, high above it, its wing-tips seemed to reach from rock to rock. I knew that this was an illusion and that the wings had ample room; that the boys who shoot their planes under the arch of a bridge, or through the Yangtze gorges, had the same exuberant glee as the boys below me were doubtless experiencing; yet if mist had suddenly swept down, that passage between the crags would have been most perilous. And even in the brief time needed to negotiate a plane through the Lairig, mist might well descend in this region of swift and unpredictable change. I have experienced this. Out of a blue sky cloud has rushed on the mountain, obliterating the world. The second time I climbed Ben MacDhui I saw this happen.

I had driven to Derry Lodge one perfect morning in June with two gentlemen who, having arrived there, were bent on returning at once to Braemar, when a car came up with four others, obviously setting out for Ben MacDhui. In a flash I had accosted them to ask if I might share their car back to Braemar in the evening: my intention was to go up, the rag-tag and bob-tail of their company, keeping them in sight but not joining myself on to them. The request was granted and I turned back to say farewell to my former companions. When

I turned again, the climbers had disappeared. I hastened after them, threading my way through the scattered pines that lie along the stream, but failing to overtake them and hurrying a little more. At last I got beyond the trees, and in all the bare glen ahead, I could see no human being. I could not believe that four people could have walked so fast as to be completely out of sight, for my own pace had been very fair. Prudence I had only once before been on a Cairngorm told me to wait; I had begun to suspect I had out-distanced my company. But I couldn't wait. The morning was cloudless and blue, it was June, I was young. Nothing could have held me back. Like a spurt of fire licking the hill, up I ran. The Etch-achan tumbled out from under snow, the summit was like wine. I saw a thousand summits at once, clear and sparkling. Then far off to the south I saw a wall of cloud like a foaming breaker. It rolled on swiftly, blotting out a hundred summits a minute – very soon it would blot out mine. I threw a hasty glance around, to fix my bearings, and pelted down towards the ruined surveyors' hut, from which the path downwards by Coire Etchachan is clearly marked by cairns; but before I reached it I was swallowed up. The whole business, from my first glimpse of the cloud to the moment it washed over me, occupied less than four minutes. Half a mile down, drinking tea in the driving mist by the side of the path, I found my lost company still ascending. On another occasion, seated by a summit cairn, gazing through a cloudless sky at peaks and lochs, I found myself unable to name some of the features I was looking at, and bent close over the map to find them out. When I raised my head, I was alone in the universe with a few blocks of red granite. This swiftness of the mist is one of its deadliest features, and the wreckage of aeroplanes, left to rust in lonely corners of the mountains, bears witness to its dreadful power.

Man's touch is on the beast creation too. He has driven the snow bunting from its nesting-sites, banished the capercailzie and re-introduced it from abroad. He has protected the grouse and all but destroyed the peregrine. He tends the red deer and exterminates the wild cat. He maintains, in fact, the economy of the red deer's life, and the red deer is at the heart of a human economy that covers this mountain mass and its surrounding glens. There are signs that this economy is cracking, and though the economy of the shooting estate is one for which I have little sympathy, I am aware that a turn of the wrist does not end it. The deer himself might perish from our mountains if man ceased to kill him; or degenerate if left to his wild; and on the crofts and small hill-farms wrested from the heather and kept productive by unremitting labour, the margin between a living and a sub-living may be decided by the extra wage of ghillie or under-keeper. Without that wage, or its equivalent in some other guise, the hill croft might well revert to heather.

These crofts and farms and gamekeepers' cottages breed men of character. They are individualists, gritty, tough, *thrawn*, intelligent, full of prejudice, with strange kinks and a salted sense of humour. Life here is hard and astringent, but it seldom kills grace in the soul. The best of them are people of many skills, inventive at supplying their needs, knowledgeable on their own ground and interested in a number of things outside it. They are not servile but avoid angering the laird; upright, though 'the Birkie up yonder' comes near enough to the thought most of them hold of God; hospitable, but never 'senseless ceevil', keeping a cool sense of proportion over what matters: though there are exceptions, to be sure, as where wouldn't there be? – a man who 'wouldna part wi' a yowie (fir cone) off his grun'', or a woman who has 'put her eyes on my lustre jug', or again a generosity that will have sugar in your cup whether you want it or not, 'to take the wildness off the tea'.

Life has not much margin here. Work goes on from dark to dark. The hay is brought in in August, the oats (with luck) in October: but at Christmas they may still stand, sodden and black in the tilted fields. And one night, before you know it, stags may have broken in and ravaged the growing crops. The crofter's wife can't go to her brother's funeral in January, because the cows are beginning to go dry and if a stranger milks them they may cease to yield altogether, and there's the income gone and milk to be bought *forbye*. The water must be carried from the well, through drifted snow or slush, unless the crofter himself has ingenuity and useful hands, and has brought his own water supply from the hill to the house; and even then it must be watched and tended through the rigours of a mountain winter.

Sometimes there is no well – no spring rises within reach of the house, but all the water to be used must be carried from the burn, up steep and toilsome banks. Then the washing is done in the centuries-old fashion, down at the foot of the banks in the burn itself – sometimes on a windy day I have seen smoke rising, and caught the wink of fire, and coming near seen a great cauldron in a sheltered nook beside the burn and figures of women moving around it.

In these crannies of the mountains, the mode of supplying elemental needs is still slow, laborious and personal. To draw your water from the well, not even a pump between you and its sparkling transparency, to break the sticks you have gathered from the wood and build your fire and set your pot upon it – there is a deep pervasive satisfaction in these simple acts. Whether you give it conscious thought or not, you are touching life, and something within you knows it. A sense of profound contentment floods me as I stoop to dip the pail. But I am aware all the same that by so living I am slowing down the tempo of life; if I had to do these things every day and all the time I should be shutting the door on other activities and interests; and I can understand why the young people resent it.

Not all the young want to run away. Far from it. Some of them love these wild places with devotion and ask nothing better than to spend their lives in them. These inherit their fathers' skills and sometimes enlarge them. Others are restive, they resent the primitive conditions of living, despise the slow ancient ways, and think that praising them is sentimentalism. These clear out. They take, however, the skills with them (or some of them do), and discover in the world outside how to graft new skills of many kinds on to their own good brier roots. An unfortunate proportion want white-collar occupations, and lose their parents' many-sidedness. For the young are like the old, various as human nature has always been, and will go on being, and life up here is full of loves, hates, jealousies, tendernesses, loyalties and betrayals, like anywhere else, and a great deal of plain humdrum happiness.

To the lovers of the hills whom they allow to share their

houses these people extend the courtesy that accepts you on equal terms without ceremonial. You may come and go at your own times. You may sit by the kitchen fire through the howling winter dark, while they stamp in from the byre in *luggit* bonnets battered with snow. They respect, whether they share it or not, your passion for the hill. But I have not found it true, as many people maintain, that those who live beside the mountains do not love them. I shall never forget the light in a boy's face, new back from the wars and toiling by his father's side on one of these high bare mountain farms, when I asked: well, and is Italy or Scotland the better? He didn't even answer the question, not in words, but looked aside at me, hardly pausing in his work, and his face glimmered. The women do not gad. The day's work keeps them busy, in and out and about, but though they do not climb the mountains (indeed how could they have time or energy?) they do look at them. It is not in this part of the Highlands that 'views is carnal'. 'It's a funeral or a phenomenon if I'm out,' says one gamekeeper's wife, but in her youth she ran on the mountains and something of their wildness is still in her speech. But even within families there are differences. Of two sisters, brought up on the very precinct of the mountain, one says 'None of your hills for me, I have seen too much of them all my days,' while the other had spent weeks on end in a small tent on the very plateau. One of the truest hill-lovers I have known was old James Downie of Braemar, whose hand-shake (given with a ceremonial solemnity) sealed my first day on Ben MacDhui. Downie had once the task of guiding Gladstone to the Pools of Dee, which the statesman decided must be visited. Now the path to the Pools, from the Braemar end, is long though not rough, shut in except for the mountain sides of the Lairig Ghru itself; and the Pools lie beneath the summit of the Pass, so that to see the wide view open on to Speyside and the hills beyond, one must climb another half mile among boulders. Gladstone refused absolutely to stir a step beyond the Pools. And Downie, the paid guide, must stop there too; an injury which Downie, the hillman, never forgave. Resentment was still raw in his voice as he told me about it, forty years later.

But while they accept mountain climbing, and are tolerant to oddities like night prowling and sleeping in the open ('You would think you were born in a cart-shed, where there wasna a door' – and when one rainy summer night we did actually set our camp beds in the cart-shed, what fun they had at us, what undisguised and hearty laughter), yet for irresponsibility they have no tolerance at all. They have only condemnation for winter climbing. They know only too well how swiftly a storm can blow up out of a clear sky, how soon the dark comes down, and how terrific the force of a hurricane can be upon the plateau; and they speak with a bitter realism of the young fools who trifle with human life by disregarding the warnings they are given. Yet if a man does not come back, they go out to search for him with patience, doggedness and skill, often in appalling weather conditions; and when there is no more hope of his being alive, seek persistently for the body. It is then that one discovers that shopmen and railway clerks and guards and sawmillers may be experienced hillmen. Indeed, talking to all sorts of people met by chance upon the hill, I realise how indiscriminately the bug of mountain feyness attacks. There are addicts in all classes of this strange pleasure. I have talked on these chance encounters with many kinds, from a gaunt scion of ancient Kings (or so he looked), with eagle beak and bony knees, descending on us out of a cloud on Ben MacDhui, kilt and Highland cloak flapping in the rain, to a red-headed greaser, an old mole-catcher, and an errand boy from Glasgow.

Many forceful and gnarled personalities, bred of the bone of the mountain, from families who have lived nowhere else, have vanished since I first began climbing here – Maggie Gruer, that granite boss, shapely in feature as a precipice, witty, acrid when it was needed, hospitable, ready for any emergency, living with a glow and a gusto that made porridge at Maggie's more than merely food. Day or night, it was all one to Maggie – no climber was turned away who would sleep on a landing, in a shed, anywhere where a human body could be laid. Nor did she scruple to turn a man out of that first deep slumber of the night, the joyous release of an exhausted body, to give his bed to a lady benighted and trudging in at one in the morning. James Downie – short, sturdy figure, erect to the last, with a hillman's dignity in his carriage; teller of stout tales – of a prince, a statesman, a professor, measuring themselves against his hill-craft; the first women to climb under his guidance, in trailing skirts and many petticoats; the hill ponies he hired for them from a taciturn shepherd who hid in his shanty and gave no help in seating 'the ladies' – 'I likit fine to see you settin' them on the shalts' – the stern discipline he exacted from his lady climbers. Indeed there was a stern and intractable root in this old man. Some of his stories were very funny, but he did not laugh much. The stern grandeur of the corries had invaded his soul. There was nothing tender or domestic about him; unmarried, he *bothied* by choice

85

in the bothy of his own croft, leaving the house to his sisters. 'He's nae couthy wi' the beasts,' his nephew's wife confided to me once. ''Deed, he's real cruel to them whiles.' The last time I stayed on the croft, during his lifetime, he insisted on carrying my bag all the way to the bus. I remonstrated, but was treated as I suppose he treated his lady climbers long before. 'I shall not do it again,' he said. 'I shall not see you again.' He was dead a few months later.

Then Sandy Mackenzie, the mighty gamekeeper on the Rothiemurchus side, already a done old man when I knew him, warming his body in the sun; and his second wife, Big Mary, surviving him for many years, dying at ninety, half-blind but indomitable. Tall, gaunt and stooped, her skin runkled and blackened from the *brook* of her open fire, her grey hair tousled in the blowing wind, she had a sybilline, an *eldritch* look on her. When I saw her last, a step-daughter had taken her from the lonely cottage, that I had shared so often – had tended her, washed her grey hair to a pure fleece of white, scrubbed her nails and her hands that were soft now because she could no longer heave her great axe or *rug* fir-roots from the ground, and dressed her in orderly black, with a lacy white shawl on her shoulders. it took my breath away; she was too exquisite – a spectacle; but the earthy and tempestuous was her truer element. She belonged there, and knew it. 'I was never one for the housecraft,' she told me once. 'I liked the outdoor work best, and the beasts.' Alone there with her ageing husband, she talked to the hens, to the old horse and to the cow, in the Gaelic that was her mother tongue. When the old man died, the cow was taken to the farm across the moor. 'May there be no more Whitewell cows here,' said the woman who milked her. 'We have not the time to be speaking to them, and will she let down the milk without you speak?'

Sometimes, as her sight failed on her, the loneliness oppressed her, for she had an avid interest in other people's lives, and books could no longer fill her need. 'The news will be sour on me before I will be hearing it,' she would complain. And she turned the news about upon her tongue – of one, 'she's a bad brat', of an infatuated man, 'he doesna see daylight but through her'; of a widower, 'it put the quietness on him, losing Mary.' For the few weeks of the year that we over-ran her cottage, she was as full of glee as we were ourselves – teased us and joked with us, though her passionate interest in every detail of our lives was never ill-mannered: she understood reticence. And the morning we left, while we collected 'meth' stove and frying-pan, and stuffed the sleeping bags and folded the camp-beds, she would send the flames crackling up the great open chimney to boil the kettle for our last ritual cup of tea; and the tears were standing in her eyes. Her hunger for folk, all the waywardness and oddity of their lives, was unappeasable. Yet, when the laird offered her a couple of rooms in another cottage, shut in and low-lying, but among people, she would have none of it. The long swoop of moor and the glittering precipices, the sweep of air around her dwelling, held her in spite of herself. I am glad that she died in her own house, between a winter with one friend and a winter with another. One blustering late September day I stepped off the train at Aviemore, to be met at once by my friend Adam Sutherland the guard. 'Do you know what has happened now? They are burying Big Mary at one o'clock.' I was in time to walk the two or three miles to the ancient kirkyard, dank among trees by the river, and to follow the men who carried the coffin down the long wet path from the road. Someone (whom I bless) had made a wreath for her, from heather and rowan berries, oats and barley and juniper, the things she saw and handled day by day. Close by lies Farquhar Shaw, survivor of the famous fight on the Inches of Perth, who troubled the neighbourhood so that when he was dead they set five heavy stone *kebbucks* upon his flat tombstone, to keep him under. I like to think that she lies near him, who was of as strong and stubborn an earth as he.

For, yes, she troubled her neighbourhood, as he did his, if on a smaller scale. Not in an evil way: there was no malice in her. But she was salt and salt can be harsh. She was *thrawn* as Auld Nick, and only God (so they tell me) can turn him aside from what he wants to do. That she set problems for those with whose lives hers was interlaced I can well believe. But she had her own integrity, rich and bountiful. I feel that I want to say of her, as Sancho Panza, challenged to find reasons for continuing to follow his master, of Don Quixote: 'I can do no otherwise . . . I have eaten his bread; I love him.'

For the living – those who have instructed me, and harboured me, and been my friends in my journey into the mountain – there are some among the many[1] whom I must name: the other Mackenzies of Whitewell, old Sandy's family, and the Mackenzies of Tullochgrue; and most especially Mrs Sutherland, Adam's wife, herself a Macdonald rooted in the place, a woman generous as the sun, who has cherished my goings and my comings for quarter of a century; and James Downie's nephew Jim McGregor, and his wife, friends to thank heaven for, who on the Dee side of the mountain, as the

Sutherlands on the Spey, have given me the franchise of their home.

These people are bone of the mountain. As the way of life changes, and a new economy moulds their life, perhaps they too will change. Yet so long as they live a life close to their wild land, subject to its weathers, something of its own nature will permeate theirs. They will be marked men.

TEN

Sleep

Well, I have discovered my mountain – its weathers, its airs and lights, its singing burns, its haunted dells, its pinnacles and tarns, its birds and flowers, its snows, its long blue distances. Year by year, I have grown in familiarity with them all. But if the whole truth of them is to be told as I have found it, I too am involved. I have been the instrument of my own discovering; and to govern the stops of the instrument needs learning too. Thus the senses must be trained and disciplined, the eye to look, the ear to listen, the body must be trained to move with the right harmonies. I can teach my body many skills by which to learn the nature of the mountain. One of the most compelling is quiescence.

No one knows the mountain completely who has not slept on it. As one slips over into sleep, the mind grows limpid; the body melts; perception alone remains. One neither thinks, nor desires, nor remembers, but dwells in pure intimacy with the tangible world.

These moments of quiescent perceptiveness before sleep are among the most rewarding of the day. I am emptied of preoccupation, there is nothing between me and the earth and sky. In midsummer the north glows with light long after midnight is past. As I watch, the light comes pouring round the edges of the shapes that stand against the sky, sharpening them till the more slender have a sort of glowing insubstantiality, as though they were themselves nothing but light. Up on the plateau, light lingers incredibly far into the night, long after it has left the rest of the earth. Watching it, the mind grows incandescent and its glow burns down into deep and tranquil sleep.

Daytime sleep, too, is good. In the heat of the day, after an early start, to lie in full daylight on the summits and slip in and out of sleep is one of the sweetest luxuries in life. For falling asleep on the mountain has the delicious corollary of awaking. To come up out of the blank of sleep and open one's eyes on scaur and gully, wondering, because one had forgotten where one was, is to recapture some pristine amazement not often savoured. I do not know if it is a common experience (certainly it is unusual in my normal sleep), but when I fall asleep out of doors, perhaps because outdoor sleep is deeper than normal, I awake with an empty mind. Consciousness of where I am comes back quite soon, but for one startled moment I have looked at a familiar place as though I had never seen it before.

Such sleep may last for only a few minutes, yet even a single minute serves this end of uncoupling the mind. It would be merely fanciful to suppose that some spirit or emanation of the mountain had intention in thus absorbing my consciousness, so as to reveal itself to a naked apprehension difficult otherwise to obtain. I do not ascribe sentience to the mountain; yet at no other moment am I sunk quite so deep into its life. I have let go my self. The experience is peculiarly precious because it is impossible to coerce.

A 4 am start leaves plenty of time for these hours of quiescence, and perhaps of sleep, on the summits. One's body is limber with the sustained rhythm of mounting, and relaxed in the ease that follows the eating of food. One is as tranquil as the stones, rooted far down in their immobility. The soil is no more a part of the earth. If sleep comes at such a moment, its coming is a movement as natural as day. And after – ceasing to be a stone, to be the soil of the earth, opening eyes that have human cognisance behind them upon what one has been so profoundly a part of. That is all. One has been in.

Once, however, I fell asleep where I would not have chosen to do so. We were on Braeriach. It was a day with hazed horizons and a flat view that had little life or interest; so we lay on our faces just beyond the summit, as near to the edge as we dared, our bodies safe to the earth, and looked down into Coire Brochain. The burns were full and everywhere there was the noise of waterfalls. We watched them drop, pouring on and on over the rock faces. Far below us on the floor of the hollow, deer were feeding, small moving specks. We watched them move. Then the sun came out and warmed us, and the pattern of movement and sound made us drowsy. Then abruptly I awoke and found myself staring down black walls of rock to a bottom incredibly remote. It is actually, I believe, some 2000 feet from the summit to the bed of the burn below; to the bottom of the inner corrie, where the deer were still feeding, is not much over a thousand; but to that

1. Those named are now, with the exception of Carrie, daughter of Sandy Mackenzie, all dead, but their descendants live on.

first horrified stare, dissociated from all thought and all memory, sensation purely, the drop seemed inordinate. With a gasp of relief I said 'Coire Brochain,' turned round on my back, eased myself from the edge, and sat up. I had looked into the abyss.

If the depth of its insensibility is the boon of daytime sleep on the mountain, nights under the sky are most delectable when the sleep is light. I like it to be so light that I am continually coming to the surface of awareness and sinking back again, just seeing, not bedevilled with thought, but living in the clear simplicity of the senses. I have slept in the open as early as May and as late as the first week in October, a time when, in our odd and unbalanced climate, there is usually a splash of radiant weather.

My one October night without a roof was bland as silk, with a late moon rising in the small hours and the mountains fluid as loch water under a silken dawn: a night of the purest witchery, to make one credit all the tales of *glamourie* that Scotland tries so hard to refute and cannot. I don't wonder. Anyone caught out of doors at four or five on such a morning would start spelling wrong. *Faerie* and *glamourie* and *witcherie* are not for men who lie in bed till eight. Find an October night warm enough to sleep out, and a dawn all mixed up with moonshine, and you will see that I am right. You too will be mis-spelled.

I do not like *glamourie*. It interposes something artificial between the world, which is one reality, and the self, which is another reality, though overlaid with a good many crusts of falseness and convention. And it is the fusion of these two realities that keeps life from corruption. So let us have done with spells.

Most of my nights out of doors have been simple summer nights, and I like waking often in them because the world is so beautiful then, and also because wild creatures, and birds, come close to a sleeper without suspicion. But there is an art in waking. I must come fully awake, and open my eyes without having moved. Once, sleeping in the daytime, I jerked awake, to find that a young blackbird, accustomed to feed from the hand, had been walking along my leg. He had asked for his alms in the odd throaty chuckle he affected, too deep in pitch to penetrate my sleep. And once a chaffinch touched my breast. In both these cases I was so lightly asleep that I felt the contact and was awake in time to catch the startled flight of my visitor. If only I had not been such a fool as to jump! But then my sleep had been broken. No, it must be a natural awakening: my eyes were closed, and now they are open, nothing more than that; and ten yards away from me a red deer is feeding in the dawn light. He moves without a sound. The world is entirely still. I too am still. Or am I? Did I move? He lifts his head, his nostrils twitch, we look at each other. Why did I let him meet my eyes? He is off. But not for far. He checks in his flight and eyes me again. This time I do not look at him. After a while he drops his head, reassured, and goes on feeding.

Sometimes I have floated up from sleep at dawn, and seen a roe, and sunk back into sleep again before my conscious mind had registered the thing. The glimpse remains a vision, wholly true, although I could not swear to it in court. When I wake for good that morning I have forgotten it. Later in the day the thought teases at the edges of my brain – *But did I dream that roe?* – and because I can't be sure it haunts me for a long time.

Or the paling below my sleeping place may be alive with finches. I have counted twenty of them when I opened my eyes. Or tits, turning themselves about in the engaging way these morsels have. Of all the tit family the one who does this to perfection is the rarest of them, the tiny crested tit, whom I have seen more than once showing himself about, now back, now front, now side, keeping each pose for a moment before flirting to a new one on a higher or a lower twig. A finished mannequin.

At other times the ear awakens first. Snipe are drumming. Then I sit up in the bag and search the sky to see the lovely downward swoop. Sometimes it is still too dark (even in a Scots midsummer) to see the pattern of movement, only the zooming fall hangs on the ear.

Out of sleep too I have heard the roaring of stags; but these are no longer outdoor nights. The nights then are cold and dark, and the roaring is fearsome as it comes from the hills that are usually so silent. The silence may be broken by another roaring. When the snows melt, cataracts sound in my ears all night, pouring through my sleep; and after many days of rain I have waked to hear the burns come down in spate, with a duller and more persistent roar than that of the stags, but in its own way as fearsome.

ELEVEN

The Senses

Having disciplined mind and body to quiescence, I must discipline them also to activity. The senses must be used. For the ear, the most vital thing that can be listened to here is silence. To bend the ear to silence is to discover how seldom it is there. Always something moves. When the air is quite still, there is always running water; and up here that is a sound one can hardly lose, though on many stony parts of the plateau one is above the watercourses. But now and then comes an hour when the silence is all but absolute, and listening to it one slips out of time. Such a silence is not a mere negation of sound. It is like a new element, and if water is still sounding with a low far-off murmur, it is no more than the last edge of an element we are leaving, as the last edge of land hangs on the mariner's horizon. Such moments come in mist, or snow, or a summer night (when it is too cool for the clouds of insects to be abroad), or a September dawn. In September dawns I hardly breathe – I am an image in a ball of glass. The world is suspended there, and I in it.

Once, on a night of such clear silence, long past midnight, lying awake outside the tent, my eyes on the plateau where an afterwash of light was lingering, I heard in the stillness a soft, an almost imperceptible thud. It was enough to make me turn my head. There on the tent pole a tawny owl stared down at me. I could just discern his shape against the sky. I stared back. He turned his head about, now one eye upon me, now the other, then melted down into the air so silently that had I not been watching him I could not have known he was gone. To have heard the movement of the midnight owl – that was rare, it was a minor triumph.

Bird song, and the noises birds make that are not singing, and the small sounds of their movements, are for the ear to catch. If there is one bird-call more than another that for me embodies the spirit of the mountain, it is the cry of the golden plover running in the bare and lonely places.

But the ear can listen also to turmoil. Gales crash into the Garbh Choire with the boom of angry seas: one can hear the air shattering itself upon rock. Cloud-bursts batter the earth and roar down the ravines, and thunder reverberates with a prolonged and menacing roll in the narrow trough of Loch Avon. Mankind is sated with noise; but up here, this naked, this elemental savagery, this infinitesimal cross-section of sound from the energies that have been at work for aeons in the universe, exhilarates rather than destroys.

Each of the senses is a way in to what the mountain has to give. The palate can taste the wild berries, blaeberry, 'wild free-born cranberry' and, most subtle and sweet of all, the avern or cloudberry, a name like a dream. The juicy gold globe melts against the tongue, but who can describe a flavour? The tongue cannot give it back. One must find the berries, golden-ripe, to know their taste.

So with the scents. All the aromatic and heady fragrances

– pine and birch, bog myrtle, the spicy juniper, heather and the honey-sweet orchis, and the clean smell of wild thyme – mean nothing at all in words. They are there, to be smelled. I am like a dog – smells excite me. On a hot moist midsummer day, I have caught a rich fruity perfume rising from the mat of grass, moss and wild berry bushes that covers so much of the plateau. The earthy smell of moss, and the soil itself, is best savoured by grubbing. Sometimes the rank smell of deer assails one's nostril, and in the spring the sharp scent of fire.

But eye and touch have the greatest potency for me. The eye brings infinity into my vision. I am lying on my back, while over me huge cumuli tear past upon a furious gale. But beyond them, very far away, in a remote pure sky, there float pale exquisite striations of cloud that can hardly be detected. I close one eye and they recede, only with both eyes open do they come into sharp enough focus for me to be sure that they are there. So now I know that the mountain makes its own wind, for these pale striae float almost motionless, while still the gale above my head drives the monstrous cumuli on. It is the eye that discovers the mystery of light, not only the moon and the stars and the vast splendours of the Aurora, but the endless changes the earth itself undergoes under changing lights. And that again, I perceive, is the mountain's own doing, for its own atmosphere alters the light. Now scaur and gully take on a gloss, now they shimmer, now they are stark – like a painting without perspective, in which objects are depicted all on one plane and of the same size, they fill the canvas and there is neither foreground nor background. Now there are sky-blue curves on the water as it slides over stones, now an impenetrable tarry blackness, slightly silvered like tar. The naked birches, if I face the sun, look black, a shining black, fine carved ebony. But if the sun is behind me it penetrates a red cloud of twigs and picks out vividly the white trunks, as though the cloud of red were behind the trunks. In a dry air, the hills shrink, they look far off and innocent; but in a moisture-laden air they charge forward, insistent and enormous, and in mist they have a nightmare quality. This is not only because I cannot see where I am going, but because the small portion of earth that I do see is isolated from its familiar surroundings, and I do not recognise it. Nothing is so ghostly as mist over snow. On a March day, I am climbing into the corrie that holds Loch Dubh; the snows have melted from the lower slopes and the burns are turbulent. They can be crossed only on snow bridges, levels of snow down which runs a sagging uneven line that shows where the water is pouring underneath. Further up, it is all snow. And now the cloud sinks down on me, a pale mist that washes out all the landmarks the snow had not already obliterated. Rocks loom out of it, gigantic, monstrous. The lochan below Loch Dubh seems enormous; the steep climb beyond it towers upwards so giddily into nothingness that I am assailed by fear: this must be the precipice itself that I am climbing – the lochan was the loch. I have passed it and am clambering towards the cliff. I know it can't be true, but the dim white ghostliness out of which stark shapes batter at my brain has overpowered my reason. I can't go further. I scramble downwards, and the grey, rather dismal, normality below the mist has a glow of comfort.

On another misty day – a transparent mist – I saw a peregrine falcon fly out from a precipice. There were the curved and pointed wings, the rapid down-beat of the pinions. Yet I stared incredulous. I was gazing upwards at a fabulous bird. No peregrine could be of such a size. It was only when he stood still on the air, before sailing back to the crag, that I believed my own eyesight; and it was only then that I understood what Hopkins meant when he wrote:

> To see the eagle's bulk, render'd in mists
> Hang of a treble size.

Mist, oddly, can also correct the illusions of the eye. A faint mist floating in a line of hills brings out the gradations of height and of distance in what had seemed one hill: there is seen to be a near and a far. In something the same way, the reflection of land in glassy water defines and clarifies its points, so that relative distance and height in a tumble of hills, so deceptive to the eye, are made clear in the loch reflection.

The eye has other illusions, that depend on one's own position. Lying on my back, and looking across the Garbh Choire to the scree slopes above Loch an Uaine, I see them as horizontal; just as from immediately below it, the Lurcher seems a horizontal plain with erect rock masses rising from it. One year we pitched our tent below the curve of the hill above Tullochgrue, on the far side from the Cairngorms. We looked out on a field that ran upwards, and above it the whole line of mountains, cut off about the 2500 feet level: the intervening moor and forest had vanished. As I lay night after night outside the door of the tent, watching the last light glow upon the plateau, I had an odd sensation of being actually myself up there. My field felt the same height, I also lay bathed in the afterglow that had gone from all but the summits. Half-closing the eyes can also change the values of what I look upon. A scatter of white flowers in grass, looked at through half-closed eyes, blaze out with a sharp clarity as though they had actually risen up out of their background. Such illusions, depending on how the eye is placed and used, drive home the truth that our habitual vision of things is not necessarily right: it is only one of an infinite number, and to glimpse an unfamiliar one, even for a moment, unmakes us, but steadies us again. It's queer but invigorating. It will take a long time to get to the end of a world that behaves like this if I do no more than turn round on my side or my back.

Other delights the eye can catch – quick moments that pass and are gone for ever: spray blown like smoke from a mountain loch in a gale; a green gleam on the snow where I know a loch lies, caught before I can see the water itself; Loch Avon, glimpsed on a rainy day from the side of the rocky burn above it, as deep a green as Loch an Uaine itself; a rainbow wavering and flickering, formed on a small shower blown by a furious wind; the air quivering above sun-filled hollows on drowsy summer afternoons; a double rainbow, dark sky in between, arched over the river, its reflection stretching from bank to bank.

How can I number the worlds to which the eye gives me entry? – the world of light, of colour, of shape, of shadow: of mathematical precision in the snowflake, the ice formation, the quartz crystal, the patterns of stamen and petal: of rhythm in the fluid curve and plunging line of the mountain faces. Why some blocks of stone, hacked into violent and tortured shapes, should so profoundly tranquillise the mind I do not know. Perhaps the eye imposes its own rhythm on what is only a confusion: one has to look creatively to see this mass of rock as more than jag and pinnacle – as beauty. Else why did men for so many centuries think mountains repulsive? A certain kind of consciousness interacts with the mountain-forms to create this sense of beauty. Yet the forms must be there for the eye to see. And forms of a certain distinction: mere dollops won't do it. It is, as with all creation, matter impregnated with mind: but the resultant issue is a living spirit, a glow in the consciousness, that perishes when the glow is dead. It is something snatched from non-being, that shadow which creeps in on us continuously and can be held off by continuous creative act. So, simply to look on anything, such as a mountain, with the love that penetrates to its essence, is to widen the domain of being in the vastness of non-being. Man has no other reason for his existence.

Touch is the most intimate sense of all. The whole sensitive skin is played upon, the whole body, braced, resistant, poised, relaxed, answers to the thrust of forces incomparably stronger than itself. Cold spring water stings the palate, the throat tingles unbearably; cold air smacks the back of the mouth, the lungs crackle. Wind blows a nostril in, one breathes on one side only, the cheek is flattened against the gum, the breath comes gaspingly, as in a fish taken from water – man is not in his element in air that moves at this velocity. Frost stiffens the muscles of the chin, mist is clammy on the cheek, after rain I run my hand through juniper or birches for the joy of the wet drops trickling over the palm, or walk through long heather to feel its wetness on my naked legs.

The hands have an infinity of pleasure in them. When I was a girl, a charming old gentlewoman said something to me that I have never forgotten. I was visiting her country home, and after lunch, going for a walk with her niece, I picked up my gloves from the hall table where I had laid them down. She took them from me and laid them back on the table. 'You don't need these. A lot of strength comes to us through the hands.' Sensation also. The feel of things, textures, surfaces, rough things like cones and bark, smooth things like stalks and feathers and pebbles rounded by water, the teasing of gossamers, the delicate tickle of a crawling caterpillar, the scratchiness of lichen, the warmth of the sun, the sting of hail, the blunt blow of tumbling water, the flow of wind – nothing that I can touch or that touches me but has its own identity for the hand as much as for the eye.

And for the foot as well. Walking barefoot has gone out of fashion since Jeanie Deans trudged to London, but no country child grows up without its benediction. Sensible people are reviving the habit. They tell me a tale up here of a gentleman in one of the shooting lodges who went to the hill barefoot: when he sat down for lunch the beaters crowded as near as they dared to see what manner of soles such a prodigy could have. But actually walking barefoot upon heather is not so grim as it sounds. I have covered odd miles myself here and there in this fashion. It begins with a burn that must be forded: once my shoes are off, I am loth to put them on again. If there are grassy flats beside my burn, I walk on over them, rejoicing in the feel of the grass to my feet; and when the grass gives place to heather, I walk on still. By setting the foot sideways to the growth of the heather, and pressing the sprays down, one can walk easily enough. Dried mud flats, sun-warmed, have a delicious touch, cushioned and smooth; so has long grass at morning, hot in the sun, but still cool and wet when the foot sinks into it, like food melting to a new flavour in the mouth. And a flower caught by the stalk between the toes is a small enchantment.

In fording a swollen stream, one's strongest sensation is of the pouring strength of the water against one's limbs; the effort to poise the body against it gives significance to this simple act of walking through running water. Early in the season the water may be so cold that one has no sensation except of cold; the whole being retracts itself, uses all its resources to endure this icy delight. But in heat the freshness of the water slides over the skin like shadow. The whole skin has this delightful sensitivity; it feels the sun, it feels the wind running inside one's garment, it feels water closing on it as one slips under – the catch in the breath, like a wave held back, the glow that releases one's entire cosmos, running to the ends of the body as the spent wave runs out upon the sand. This plunge into the cold water of a mountain pool seems for a brief moment to disintegrate the very self; it is not to be borne: one is lost: stricken: annihilated. Then life pours back.

TWELVE

Being

Here then may be lived a life of the senses so pure, so untouched by any mode of apprehension but their own, that the body may be said to think. Each sense heightened to its most exquisite awareness is in itself total experience. This is the innocence we have lost, living in one sense at a time to live all the way through.

So there I lie on the plateau, under me the central core of fire from which was thrust this grumbling grinding mass of plutonic rock, over me blue air, and between the fire of the rock and the fire of the sun, scree, soil and water, moss, grass, flower and tree, insect, bird and beast, wind, rain and snow – the total mountain. Slowly I have found my way in. If I had other senses, there are other things I should know. It is nonsense to suppose, when I have perceived the exquisite division of running water, or a flower, that my separate senses can make, that there would be nothing more to perceive were we but endowed with other modes of perception. How could we imagine flavour, or perfume, without the senses of taste and smell? They are completely unimaginable. There must be many exciting properties of matter that we cannot know because we have no way to know them. Yet, with what we

have, what wealth! I add to it each time I go to the mountain
– the eye sees what it didn't see before, or sees in a new way
what it had already seen. So the ear, the other senses. It is
an experience that grows; undistinguished days add their part,
and now and then, unpredictable and unforgettable, come the
hours when heaven and earth fall away and one sees a new
creation. The many details – a stroke here, a stroke there –
come for a moment into perfect focus, and one can read at
last the word that has been from the beginning.

These moments come unpredictably, yet governed, it would
seem, by a law whose working is dimly understood. They come
to me most often, as I have indicated, waking out of outdoor
sleep, gazing tranced at the running of water and listening to
its song, and most of all after hours of steady walking, with
the long rhythm of motion sustained until motion is felt, not
merely known by the brain, as the 'still centre' of being. In
some such way I suppose the controlled breathing of the Yogi
must operate. Walking thus, hour after hour, the senses keyed,
one walks the flesh transparent. But no metaphor, *transparent*,
or *light as air*, is adequate. The body is not made negligible,
but paramount. Flesh is not annihilated but fulfilled. One is
not bodiless, but essential body.

It is therefore when the body is keyed to its highest poten-
tial and controlled to a profound harmony deepening into
something that resembles trance, that I discover most nearly
what it is *to be*. I have walked out of the body and into the
mountain. I am a manifestation of its total life, as is the starry
saxifrage or the white-winged ptarmigan.

So I have found what I set out to find. I set out on my
journey in pure love. It began in childhood, when the stormy

violet of a gully on the back of Sgoran Dubh, at which I used to gaze from a shoulder of the Monadhliaths, haunted my dreams. That gully, with its floating, its almost tangible ultra-marine, *thirled* me for life to the mountain. Climbing Cairngorms was then for me a legendary task, which heroes, not men, accomplished. Certainly not children. It was still legendary on the October day, blue, cold and brilliant after heavy snow, when I climbed Creag Dhubh above Loch an Eilein, alone and expectant. I climbed like a child stealing apples, with a fearful look behind. The Cairngorms were forbidden country – this was the nearest I had come to them; I was delectably excited. But how near to them I was coming I could not guess, as I toiled up the last slope and came out above Glen Einich. Then I gulped the frosty air – I could not contain myself, I jumped up and down, I laughed and shouted. There was the whole plateau, glittering white, within reach of my fingers, an immaculate vision, sun-struck, lifting against a sky of dazzling blue. I drank and drank. I have not yet done drinking that draught. From that hour I belonged to the Cairn-gorms, though – for several reasons – it was a number of years until I climbed them.

So my journey into an experience began. It was a journey always for fun, with no motive beyond that I wanted it. But at first I was seeking only sensuous gratification – the sensa-tion of height, the sensation of movement, the sensation of speed, the sensation of distance, the sensation of effort, the sensation of ease: the lust of the flesh, the lust of the eyes, the pride of life. I was not interested in the mountain for itself, but for its effect upon me, as puss caresses not the man but herself against the man's trouser leg. But as I grew older, and less self-sufficient, I began to discover the mountain in itself. Everything became good to me, its contours, its colours, its waters and rock, flowers and birds. This process has taken many years, and is not yet complete. Knowing another is endless. And I have discovered that man's experience of them enlarges rock, flower and bird. The thing to be known grows with the knowing.

I believe that I now understand in some small measure why the Buddhist goes on pilgrimage to a mountain. The journey is itself part of the technique by which the god is sought. It is a journey into Being; for as I penetrate more deeply into the mountain's life, I penetrate also into my own. For an hour I am beyond desire. It is not ecstasy, that leap out of the self that makes man like a god. I am not out of myself, but in myself. I am. To know Being, this is the final grace accorded from the mountain.

A BED. A BOOK. A MOUNTAIN.

by Jeanette Winterson

I am lying in bed reading Nan Shepherd's *The Living Mountain*. This is a kind of geo-poetic exploration of the Cairngorms – a mountain range in north-east Scotland. The book was written in the 1940s, and lay unpublished until the 1970s. Now it has been reissued by Canongate.

Reading it seems to me to explain why reading is so important. And odd. And necessary. And not like anything else.

There is no substitute for reading.

To go back to the book.

Nan Shepherd never married and never lived anywhere but her native Scotland in a village at the foot of the Cairngorms. She was well educated and well travelled, but she always came home. She loved the Cairngorms. She wrote, 'The mind cannot carry away all it has to give, nor does it always believe possible what it has carried away.'

I am not a mountain climber or even a hillwalker. I know nothing about the Cairngorms. The book was sent to me and because books and doors both need to be opened, I opened it. A book is a door; on the other side is somewhere else.

I found myself wandering the mountain range in the

company of Nan Shepherd. She is dead, but that doesn't make any difference. Her voice is as clear and fast-flowing as the streams she follows to their source, only to find that the source always points inwards, further. There is always further to go.

I like it that I can lie in bed and read a book about mountain climbing. There are two dominant modes of experience offered to us at present – actual (hence our appetite for reality TV, documentaries and 'true-life' drama) and virtual – the Web. Sometimes these come together, as in the bizarre concept of Facebook: relationships without the relating.

Reading offers something else: an imaginative world.

I don't want to confuse this with fantasy or escapism. For me, the imaginative world is the total world, not a world shredded and packed into compartments. For the poet Wordsworth, the job of the poet and the poem is to 'see into the life of things'.

This cannot be done if we are only separating. Imagination allows us to experience ourselves and our world as something that is relational and interdependent. Everything exists in relation to everything else. The reason that *The Living Mountain* is a 'good' book is that it takes a very particular and tiny subject and finds in it, or pulls out of it, a story about how we can understand the world.

The book is a metaphor, yes, but it is also specifically about the Cairngorms. The opening it makes in the mind is its capacity to connect the specific and the local with the universal (and as Robert Macfarlane points out in his lovely introduction, the universal is not the same as the general).

A medium other than the book could not achieve the effect of this book nearly so well. A book lets you follow a writer's mind. Reading does not move in linear time in the way that a movie or even a radio piece does. Of course there is a beginning, a middle and an end, but in 'good' books that is irrelevant. We don't remember the books that have mattered to us by the chronology of their story-telling, but by the impression and effect of the story and of the language used to tell it. Memory is talismanic. We hold on to what we need and let the rest go. Just as in our own lives events separated in time sit side by side in memory, so the effect of a book is to let us live nearer to total time than linear time allows.

Linear time is exhausting. Life has never been more rushed. This present way of being is not a truth about life or a truth about time; it is propositional. We can disagree.

Part of Nan Shepherd's lifelong relationship with the mountain is to stop rushing to the top of the various plateaus of the Cairngorms. At first it is all about the exhilaration of the ascent. How far can she go? How fast? Then she starts circling like a dog with a good nose. She finds that she wants to be in the mountains. 'Often the mountain gives itself most completely when I have no destination, when I reach nowhere in particular, but have gone out merely to be with the mountain, as one visits a friend with no intention but to be with him.'

To cross the threshold of a book is to make a journey in total time. I don't think of reading as leisure time or wasted time and especially not as downtime. The total time of a book is more like uptime than downtime, in the way that salmon swim upstream to get home.

We have lost all sense of home – whether it's the natural world, our only planet, or our bodies, now sites of anxiety and dissatisfaction, or our scrabble for property in vast alienated cities where few can afford safety, peace, quiet, even a garden.

How can a book get me home? It reminds me of where home is – by which I mean I am remapped by the book. My internal geography shifts, my values shift. I remember myself, my world, my body, who I am.

The remapping is sometimes overwhelming – the wow factor of those books that we know have changed our territory – but usually it is much more subtle, and more of a reorienting. I feel settled in myself. To put it another way, I am a settler in myself. I inhabit my own space.

I had a rough childhood. I left home at sixteen and for the next ten years physical home was a provisional space, not permanent, rarely secure. During that time I discovered that books gave me a way of being at home in myself. They provided a shining centre – and if that sounds a bit mystical, I suppose it is, but we all have to find a way of being, a way of living, and as far as I'm concerned, life has an inside as well as an outside. Most, if not all, of our time and energy goes into life on the outside – jobs, money, status, getting and spending – and this is disorientating. And it means that if life on the outside is a mess, as it often is, or unsatisfactory, we have no inner resources to help us through.

Books work from the inside out. They are a private conversation happening somewhere in the soul.

Often then, still, now, if I can use the book as a compass I can right my way. Reading calms me and it clears my head. In the company of a book my mind expands and I find myself less anxious and more aware.

This happens in the interaction between me and any, every encounter with a book that has being. And a book that has being is a book where the writer has found something essential and can communicate it to me.

It really doesn't matter what. The Cairngorms or *Wuthering Heights*. *Cloud Atlas* or *Moby-Dick*. *Zen and the Art of Motorcycle Maintenance* or a Carol Ann Duffy poem. Poetry is all about being, and because we are much less concerned with the subject matter or the story of a poem, it is easier to understand Susan Sontag's remark, 'A work of art is not just *about* something; it *is* something.'

The is-ness of art, its being, is vital. What it is about may be interesting and absorbing, may be topical, may be urgent, but over time what comes back to us, sustains us, is none of that. Art, and that includes writing, is not an end in itself; it is a medium for the soul.

You need not believe in the gods to believe in your own soul. It is that part of you that feels not obliged to materiality. I do not know if the soul survives physical death – and I do not care – but I know that to lose your soul while you are alive is worse than death.

I want to protect my soul.

Reading isn't the only way to protect your soul, or to live in total time, or to find your own way home – but we're talking about reading here, and my most intense experience is with and through language. I am like Adam and I need to name things. This is not taxonomy and it's not reductive, rather it's trying to find a language that fits. Fits what? Not only the object or the experience but also the feeling.

It is impossible to have a thought without a feeling. Impossible not to feel. You can suppress and distort your feelings, you can displace them and be honest about them, but like it or don't like it, you are feeling something every second. Nothing mystical here. In the economy of the body, the limbic pathway takes precedence over the neural highway. We are designed and built to feel.

When I can find a language for my feelings I can own them and not be owned by them. I can be enriched as mind and emotion work together instead of against each other. Art, all art, is good at this essential relationship, but literature finds us the words we need. And we need words. Not empty information. Not babble. Not data. We need a language capable of simple, beautiful expression yet containing complex thought that yields up our feelings instead of depriving us of them.

You only get that kind of language-possibility through reading at a high level; that doesn't mean difficult or abstruse – quite the contrary. What we think of as difficult is often only unfamiliar, so it can take a bit of time to get into a book. Reading is becoming a casualty of the surf-syndrome of the Web. Reading is not skimming for information. Reading is a deeper dive.

Or a high climb.

Nan Shepherd talks about the exhilaration of altitude. The air is thinner. The body is lighter. But you have to acclimatise. You have to acclimatise yourself to books.

I am aware that reading is new. Mass literacy didn't really start until the mid-nineteenth century, and we have had an uneasy relationship with reading ever since. Lots of people don't really read and don't want to read.

I think that is to do with education and cultural expectation. There is a wonderful group called The Reader Organisation, run by Jane Davis, who is a cross between Bob Geldof and Florence Nightingale, with a bit of Nanny McPhee thrown in. Her reason for living is to take reading into places where reading does not go – prisons, housing estates, children's homes, etc. She works in Liverpool with people who have often had no real schooling. Her results are incredible. Kids calm down, guys grow up, harassed mothers find themselves mirrored in Sylvia Plath and Shakespeare. There is no dumbing down offered. Against received wisdom, by which I mean received stupidity, her crazy project works. The Reader has no direct government funding.

When I left home I didn't find hope in realistic docu-drama narratives of deprived kids with no choices or chances. I found myself in Aladdin, Huck Finn, Heathcliff, the Little Prince, Henry IV. I identified with Hotspur because of course I identify with the outsider. And soon enough I found Albert Camus. *L'Etranger*.

I should add that my father could not read without running his finger along the line and saying the words out loud very slowly. My mother was very bright but had left school at fourteen. We had no books at home, and anyway I tried not to be at home. I was always in the Pennines, where we lived.

So it is not quite true that I am not a hillwalker.

Reading was not so important to my working-class community, unless it was the Bible. Reading the Bible means that you can read anything else – and it makes Shakespeare easy because the language of the King James Version is also the language of Shakespeare. We had a strong oral tradition in the north of England, and people often forget that not being able to read, or not reading, even fifty years ago, let alone a hundred years ago, was very different from not reading now.

We live under 24/7 saturation bombing from enervated mass media and a bogus manufactured popular culture. If you don't read you will likely be watching telly, or on the computer, or listening to fake music from puppet-show bands.

When the families I knew in my northern textile town didn't read – and they didn't – they were in the brass band, or in the choir, telling their own stories down the pub or on the greyhound track, finding the quiet pleasure of mending kit or working the allotment, or walking for miles in the Pennines. I am not glamorising this working-class life; it was hard and short, and I could not stay there and I would not want it back. But it had a genuine culture of its own – roots up – and it was not force-fed adverts, consumerism and *The X Factor*.

The consequences of homogenised mass culture plus the failure of our education system and our contempt for books and art (it's either entertainment or elitist, never vital and democratic), mean that not reading cuts off the possibility of private thinking, or of a trained mind, or of a sense of self not dependent on external factors.

A trained mind is a mind that can concentrate. Attention Deficit Disorder is not a disease; it is a consequence of not reading. Teach a child to read and keep that child reading and you will change everything. And yes, I mean everything.

Back to the mountain.

Powerfully argued in *The Living Mountain* is the need to be physical, to be in the body, and to let the senses and the soul work in harmony with the mind. This seems a long way from lying in bed and reading a book. But it isn't far at all.

Reading stills the body for a while, allowing rest without torpor and quiet without passivity. Reading is not a passive act. Engaged in the book, in company with the writer, the mind can roam where it will. Such freedom to roam reminds us that body and mind both need exercise and activity, and that neither the mind nor the body can cope with confinement. And if the body has to cope with confinement, then all the more reason to have developed a mind that knows how to roam.

In the last months of her long life Nan Shepherd was in hospital, unable to climb her beloved mountains. But her mind went on climbing. She could not be trapped.

Reading is a way through, a way in, a way out. It is a way of life. The rewards are immense.

GLOSSARY

aace ashes

Ablach, tiny undersized creature

anent, over against, concerning

antrin, one here and there

a'thing, everything

aweirs o', inclined to

barkit, covered as with bark, peeled

begeck, disappointment

begrutten, tear-stained

ben the hoose, inside, further into the house or next room

besom, hussy

bide; bydin, stay, remain; staying

bike, wasps' nest

birse, vb., to force, press upwards; *n., to have one's birse up,* one's temper roused

birstled, cooked till hard and crisp

bit, little, scrap of

blake, cockroach, beetle

blate, shy, diffident

blaud, dirty, soil

blin' drift, drifting snow

blithe, happy

bog-jaaveled, completely at a loss

bourrach, small group, swarm

bow-hoched, bow-legged

brear, first small blade appearing above the ground; *brears o' the e'e,* eyelashes

broch, halo

brook, soot

brose, oatmeal and milk or hot water

buckie, limpet

bung; ta'en the bung, taken offence

byordinar, unusually

byous, beyond the ordinary

caddis, dust, fluff

ca'ed, driven

cairded, scolded

canalye, Fr. *canaille*

cantle up, brighten up

cantrip, piece of mischief

canty, lively, cheerful

cark, care

chappit, (thumb) hacked

chau'mer, chamber, bothy

chiel, lad

cloor, dent, blow

clorted, covered with mud

clout, rag

clyte, fall

collieshangie, animated talk

coorse, bad

connach, devour, spoil

contermashious, contradictory, obstinate

crack, gossip

craiturie, little creature

a crap for a' corn and a baggie for orrels, an appetite for absolutely anything and then some (literally: a bag for leftovers)

creish, fat

crined, shrunk, shrivelled

curran, a number

dambrod, chess-board

dander, to have one's dander up, temper roused

dawtie, pet, darling

deave, deafen, torment with insistence

deemie, farm, kitchenmaid

deil, devil

delvin, digging

dicht, wipe

dingin' on, raining or snowing hard

dirds, bangs (vb)

dirdums, daein' dirdums, doing great things

dirl, ring, vibrate

doit, small copper coin

dour, stubborn

dowie, spiritless

drookit, soaked, drowned

drummlie, physically upset

dubbit, covered with mud

dubs, mud

dunt, a blow

a dunt on the riggin, not all there (dent in the roof)

dwam, faint, swoon

(neither) echie nor ochie, not the smallest sound

e'en, eyes

eident, diligent

ettlin', desirous after

f=wh

fa, who

fan, when

fat, what

fairin', present from the fair

fash yersel, put yourself to trouble

faur, where

fee'd, hired

ferlies, wonders

fey, peculiar, other-worldly

ficher, fiddle, fidget

fient, never! not a! (lit: devil!)

flan, gust

fleg, fright, frighten

fleggit, startled

flinchin, deceitful promise of better weather

flist, storm of temper

foo, how

forbye, besides

forfoch'en, exhausted, fought, done
forty-fitted Janet, centipede
fou', drunk
ful, proud
fyle, soil, make dirty
gait, way
gar, cause to
geal-cauld, ice-cold
geet, child
gey, rather
a gey snod bit deemie, a rather neat
    little maid
geylies, considerable
gin, if
girn, fret
girse, grass
glower, scowl
gomeril, fool
gorbals, nestlings
graip, fork (for land work)
grat, cried
greetin, crying
guff, smell
gumption, sense, vigour, initiative
gype, stupid person
gyte, ga'en gyte, gone out of one's
    mind
haggar, clumsy hacking
halarackit, high-spirited, rowdy
    without offensiveness
halfin, teenager
hain, save, spare
hairst, harvest
hantle, a good deal
hap, cover up

havering, talking nonsense
heelster-gowdie, upside down
hine awa'/up, far away/up
hippit, stiff in the hips
hirple, limp
hive, a skin sore
hotter, boil vigorously
hotterel, a swarm
howff, draught
howk, dig
hurdies, hips
ilka, each, every
ill-fashioned, inquisitive
inen, in among
ingan, onion
jaloose, guess, suspect
jaud, (common) woman
kebbuck, cheese
keek, keeking, peek, peeking
kink-hoast, whooping-cough
kitties, calves (a pet name for)
kittled, tickled
kowk, retch
kye, cattle
lave, rest
legammachy, long story without
    much in it
leuch, laughed
lift, sky
limmer, hussy
lippen, trust
to lippen to, to trust
loon, boy, lad
louse, loosen, unharness
lousin' time, end of the working

day
lowe, blaze
lugs, ears
mavis, song thrush
mim-mou'ed, primly spoken or
   behaved
mishanter, mishap, disaster
mommets, dolls, puppets
mowse, right (with sense of Latin
   fas), *nae mowse, nefas*, uncanny
my certies, indeed (emphasis)
neips, turnips
neuk, corner
newse, chat
nieve, fist
nimsch, fragment
nippit, pinched, narrow in outlook
nowt, cattle
nyatter, nag
nyod (an exclamation, lit: God!)
ootlin, outsider, outcast
or, before
orra, odd, miscellaneous
orrels, bits and pieces
oxter, arm-pit, *vb.*, to put the arm
   round
pech, sigh
penurious, particular, ill to please
pi, pious, sanctimonious
pilgate, quarrel
pleuch, plough
pliskey, trick, escapade
pooches, pockets
preens, pins
puckle, a few

puddock, frog
pyet, magpie
pyockie, poke, bag
queets, ankles
raivelled, confused
rary, go about noisily, clamour
rax, stretch
reeshle, rustle
rickle, a structure put loosely
   together, loose heap
rive, tear asunder
roarie-bummlers, (noisy blunderers)
   storm clouds
roup, a sale or public auction
rug, pull
sair, sore
sair weary, very tired
sark, shirt
scalin', dispersing
scran, scrounge
scunnered, disgusted
scutter awa', do things slowly and
   not very thoroughly
scuttered, fiddled about
shaltie, pony
shank, stocking being knitted
sharger, half grown creature
sharn, dung
sheen, shoes
sheepy silver, flakes of mica (in a
   stone)
shog, push
sic mannie sic horsie, like master
   like man
skellochin', shrieking

skirp, splatter
sklype, clumsy worthless person
smeddum, vigour of intellect
smored, smothered (in snow)
snod, neat
sonsy, of generous proportions
sooples, supples, softens
soo's snoot, pig's nose
sotter, untidy dress
sowens, a kind of fine-meal
   porridge
spangin', walking vigorously
speir, ask
spoot-ma-gruel, any unappetising
   food
spunk, match
spurtle, a round stick for stirring
   porridge
stap, stuff
steekit, shut
stew, dust
stite, nonsense
stob, splinter under the skin
sumph, heavy lout
swacker, more supple
swage, loosen, make easy
sweir, lazy
tackie, tig (child's game)
tangle, icicle, seaweed
tansies, ragworts (plants)
teem, empty
teen, temper, mood
thirled, bound, tied
thole, endure
thraw, wring

thrawn, obstinate
thrums, scraps of thread
timmer knife, wooden knife
   (useless)
tine, loose
tinkey, tinker
trauchle, n., trouble, heavy toil
trig, neat
tyauve, struggle
wae, woeful
wantin, lacking
warstle, wrestle
waucht, draught
waur; nane the waur, worse; none
   the worse
wersch, without savour, insipid
whammlin', jogging
whiles, at the same time
whin, gorse, furze bush
wrocht, worked, laboured
yird, vb., to give a blow
yon, that
yowies, pine cones